SIMUL 2023

The Fifteenth International Conference on Advances in System Simulation

November 13th – 17th, 2023

Valencia, Spain

SIMUL 2023 Editors

Carlo Simon, Hochschule Worms, Germany

Sibylle Fröschle, Technische Universität Hamburg, Germany

Printed from e-media with permission by:

Curran Associates, Inc.
57 Morehouse Lane
Red Hook, NY 12571

Some format issues inherent in the e-media version may also appear in this print version.

Printed with permission by Curran Associates, Inc. (2024)

International Academy, Research, and Industry Association (IARIA)
412 Derby Way
Wilmington, DE 19810

Phone: (408) 893-6407
Fax: (408) 527-6351

petre@iaria.org

Additional copies of this publication are available from:

Curran Associates, Inc.
57 Morehouse Lane
Red Hook, NY 12571 USA
Phone: 845-758-0400
Fax: 845-758-2633
Email: curran@proceedings.com
Web: www.proceedings.com

Table of Contents

SIMUL 2023

Forward

The Fifteenth International Conference on Advances in System Simulation (SIMUL 2023), held on November 13 - 17, 2023 in Valencia, Spain, continued a series of events focusing on advances in simulation techniques and systems providing new simulation capabilities.

While different simulation events are already scheduled for years, SIMUL 2023 identified specific needs for ontology of models, mechanisms, and methodologies in order to make easy an appropriate tool selection. With the advent of Web Services and WEB 3.0 social simulation and human-in simulations bring new challenging situations along with more classical process simulations and distributed and parallel simulations. An update on the simulation tool considering these new simulation flavors was aimed at, too.

The conference provided a forum where researchers were able to present recent research results and new research problems and directions related to them. The conference sought contributions to stress-out large challenges in scale system simulation and advanced mechanisms and methodologies to deal with them. The accepted papers covered topics on social simulation, transport simulation, simulation tools and platforms, simulation methodologies and models, and distributed simulation.

We welcomed technical papers presenting research and practical results, position papers addressing the pros and cons of specific proposals, such as those being discussed in the standard forums or in industry consortiums, survey papers addressing the key problems and solutions on any of the above topics, short papers on work in progress, and panel proposals.

We take here the opportunity to warmly thank all the members of the SIMUL 2023 technical program committee as well as the numerous reviewers. The creation of such a broad and high quality conference program would not have been possible without their involvement. We also kindly thank all the authors that dedicated much of their time and efforts to contribute to the SIMUL 2023. We truly believe that thanks to all these efforts, the final conference program consists of top quality contributions.

This event could also not have been a reality without the support of many individuals, organizations and sponsors. We also gratefully thank the members of the SIMUL 2023 organizing committee for their help in handling the logistics and for their work that is making this professional meeting a success. We gratefully appreciate to the technical program committee co-chairs that contributed to identify the appropriate groups to submit contributions.

We hope the SIMUL 2023 was a successful international forum for the exchange of ideas and results between academia and industry and to promote further progress in simulation research. . We also hope that Valencia provided a pleasant environment during the conference and everyone saved some time for exploring this beautiful city

SIMUL 2023 Steering Committee

Carlo Simon, Hochschule Worms - University of Applied Sciences, Germany
Frank Herrmann, University of Applied Sciences Regensburg, Germany
Sibylle Fröschle, TUHH - Hamburg University of Technology, Germany

SIMUL 2023 Publicity Chair
Lorena Parra Boronat, Universitat Politecnica de Valencia, Spain
Sandra Viciano Tudela, Universitat Politecnica de Valencia, Spain
Jose Miguel Jimenez, Universitat Politecnica de Valencia, Spain

SIMUL 2023

Committee

SIMUL 2023 Steering Committee

Carlo Simon, Hochschule Worms - University of Applied Sciences, Germany
Frank Herrmann, University of Applied Sciences Regensburg, Germany
Sibylle Fröschle, TUHH - Hamburg University of Technology, Germany

SIMUL 2023 Publicity Chair

Lorena Parra Boronat, Universitat Politecnica de Valencia, Spain
Sandra Viciano Tudela, Universitat Politecnica de Valencia, Spain
Jose Miguel Jimenez, Universitat Politecnica de Valencia, Spain

SIMUL 2023 Technical Program Committee

Petra Ahrweiler, Johannes Gutenberg University Mainz, Germany
Chrissanthi Angeli, University of West Attica, Greece
Ozgur M. Araz, College of Business | University of Nebraska–Lincoln, USA
Alfonso Ariza Quintana, University of Malaga, Spain
Natesh B. Arunachalam, The University of Texas at Austin, USA
Michel Audette, Old Dominion University, USA
Ana Paula Barbosa Póvoa, Universidade de Lisboa, Portugal
Marek Bauer, Politechnika Krakowska, Poland
Sahil Belsare, Walmart / Northeastern University, USA
Massimo Bertolini, University of Modena and Reggio Emilia - UNIMORE, Italy
John Betts, Monash University, Australia
Patrick Biemelt, University of Paderborn, Germany
Maria Julia Blas, Instituto de Desarrollo y Diseño (INGAR) | UTN-CONICET, Argentina
Paolo Bocciarelli, University of Rome Tor Vergata, Italy
Stefan Bosse, University of Bremen, Germany
Jalil Boudjadar, Aarhus University, Denmark
Christos Bouras, University of Patras, Greece
Lelio Campanile, Università degli Studi della Campania "L. Vanvitelli", Italy
Yuxin Chen, University of California, Davis, USA
Franco Cicirelli, ICAR-CNR, Italy
Fábio Coelho, CEG-IST Instituto Superior Técnico | University of Lisbon, Portugal
Federico Concone, University of Palermo, Italy
Duilio Curcio, University of Calabria, Italy
Andrea D'Ambrogio, University of Roma TorVergata, Italy
Gabriele D'Angelo, University of Bologna, Italy
Luis Antonio de Santa-Eulalia, Business School | Université de Sherbrooke, Canada
Daniel Delahaye, ENAC LAB, Toulouse, France

Alexander Ditter, Friedrich-Alexander University Erlangen-Nürnberg (FAU), Germany
Anatoli Djanatliev, University of Erlangen-Nuremberg, Germany
Julie Dugdale, University Grenoble Alps, France
Mahmoud Elbattah, Université de Picardie Jules Verne, France
Sabeur Elkosantini, University of Carthage, Tunisia
Amr Eltawil, School of Innovative Design Engineering / Japan University of Science and Technology, Egypt
Diego Encinas, Informatics Research Institute LIDI - CIC - UNLP, Argentina
Fouad Erchiqui, Université du Québec en Abitibi-Témiscamingue, Canada
Zuhal Erden, Atilim University, Turkey
Mourad Fakhfakh, University of Sfax, Tunisia
Javier Faulin, Public University of Navarra, Spain
Sibylle Fröschle, University of Oldenburg, Germany
José Manuel Galán, Universidad de Burgos, Spain
Ramo Galeano, Universidad Autonoma de Barcelona, Spain
Erol Gelenbe, Institute of Theoretical and Applied Informatics of the Polish Academy of Sciences, Poland
Simon Genser, Virtual Vehicle Research GmbH, Graz, Austria
Katja Gilly de la Sierra-Llamazares, Universidad Miguel Hernández, Spain
Apostolos Gkamas, University Ecclesiastical Academy of Vella of Ioannina, Greece
Denis Gracanin, Virginia Tech, USA
Antoni Grau, Technical University of Catalonia, Barcelona, Spain
Andrew Greasley, Aston University, Birmingham, UK
Feng Gu, The College of Staten Island, CUNY, USA
Nikolos Gurney, University of Southern California | Institute for Creative Technologies, USA
Stefan Haag, University of Applied Sciences Worms, Germany
Petr Hanáček, Brno University of Technology, Czech Republic
Magdalena Hańderek, Cracow University of Technology, Poland
Thomas Hanne, University of Applied Sciences and Arts Northwestern Switzerland / Institute for Information Systems, Switzerland
Eduardo Hargreaves, Petrobras, Brazil
Frank Herrmann, University of Applied Sciences Regensburg, Germany
Tsan-sheng Hsu, Institute of Information Science | Academia Sinica, Taiwan
Xiaolin Hu, Georgia State University, Atlanta, USA
Marc-Philippe Huget, Polytech Annecy-Chambery-LISTIC | University of Savoie, France
Mauro Iacono, Università degli Studi della Campania "Luigi Vanvitelli", Italy
Lisa Jackson, Loughborough University, UK
Maria João Viamonte, Institute of Engineering (ISEP) - Polytechnic Institute of Porto (IPP), Portugal
Peter Kemper, William & Mary, USA
Yun Bae Kim, Sungkyunkwan University (SKKU), Korea
Youngjae Kim, Sogang University, Seoul, Korea
Hildegarde Koen, Council for Scientific and Industrial Research (CSIR), South Africa
Dmitry G. Korzun, Petrozavodsk State University | Institute of Mathematics and Information Technology, Russia
Mouna Kotti, University of Gabes, Tunisia
Vladik Kreinovich, University of Texas at El Paso, USA
Anatoly Kurkovsky, Georgia Gwinnett College - Greater Atlanta University System of Georgia, USA
Massimo La Scala, Politecnico di Bari, Italy
Ettore Lanzarone, University of Bergamo, Italy

Herman Le Roux, Council for Scientific and Industrial Research (CSIR), South Africa
Fedor Lehocki, Slovak University of Technology in Bratislava, Slovakia
Laurent Lemarchand, University of Brest (UBO), France
Huiye Liu, Georgia Institute of Technology, USA
António M. Lopes, University of Porto, Portugal
Fabian Lorig, Malmö University | IoTaP, Sweden
Emilio Luque, University Autonoma of Barcelona (UAB), Spain
Johannes Lüthi, University of Applied Sciences - Fachhochschule Kufstein Tirol, Austria
Imran Mahmood, Brunel University London, UK
Fahad Maqbool, University of Sargodha, Pakistan
Eda Marchetti, ISTI-CNR, Pisa, Italy
Romolo Marotta, University of Rome "Sapienza", Italy
Niels Martin, Research Foundation Flanders (FWO) - Hasselt University, Belgium
Omar Masmali, The University of Texas, El Paso, USA
Michele Mastroianni, Università degli Studi della Campania "Luigi Vanvitelli", Italy
Andrea Matta, Politecnico di Milano, Italy
Radek Matušů, Tomas Bata University in Zlin, Czech Republic
Roger McHaney, Kansas State University, USA
Nuno Melão, Polytechnic Institute of Viseu, Portugal
Roderick Melnik, MS2Discovery Interdisciplinary Research Institute | Wilfrid *Laurier* University, Canada
Adel Mhamdi, RWTH Aachen University, Germany
Owen Molloy, National University of Ireland, Galway, Ireland
Sébastien Monnet, LISTIC / Savoie Mont Blanc University, France
Federico Montori, University of Bologna, Italy
Jérôme Morio, ONERA (the French Aerospace Lab), France
Paulo Moura Oliveira, Universidade de Trás-os-Montes e Alto Douro (UTAD) / INESC-TEC Porto, Portugal
Nazmun Nahar, University of Jyvaskyla, Finland
Luis Gustavo Nardin, National College of Ireland, Ireland
Alessandro Pellegrini, Sapienza University of Rome, Italy
Tomas Potuzak, University of West Bohemia, Czech Republic
Dipak Pudasaini, Tribhuvan University, Nepal / Ryerson University, Canada
Francesco Quaglia, University of Rome Tor Vergata, Italy
Patrick Reinwald, University of Klagenfurt, Austria
Marco Remondino, Università degli Studi di Genova, Italy
Dupas Rémy, University of Bordeaux, France
Oscar Rodríguez Polo, University of Alcala, Spain
Kristin Yvonne Rozier, Iowa State University, USA
Julio Sahuquillo, Universitat Politecnica de Valencia, Spain
Ignacio Sanchez-Navarro, University of the West of Scotland, UK
Nandakishore Santhi, Los Alamos National Laboratory, USA
Victorino Sanz, ETSI Informática | UNED, Spain
Paulo Jorge Sequeira Goncalves, Instituto Politecnico de Castelo Branco, Portugal
Li Shi, Snap Inc., USA
Patrick Siarry, Université Paris-Est Créteil (UPEC), France
Carlo Simon, Hochschule Worms - University of Applied Sciences, Germany
Leszek Siwik, AGH-UST University of Science and Technology, Krakow, Poland
Yuri N. Skiba, Universidad Nacional Autónoma de México, Mexico
Azeddien M. Sllame, University of Tripoli, Libya

Copyright Information

Urban Consolidation Centers – an Analysis of Internal Processes Using Discrete Event Process Simulation

Max Wuennenberg[1], Chen Yang[1], Johannes Fottner[1]
[1]Chair of Materials Handling, Material Flow, Logistics
Technical University of Munich
Garching bei Muenchen, Germany
e-mail: {max.wuennenberg, c.yang, j.fottner}@tum.de

***Abstract*— This study addresses the spatial constraints posed by urbanization and population growth in cities. It evaluates different types of urban consolidation centers to improve urban logistics. Design parameters are identified through literature review, and an evaluation methodology is developed. Simulation models are created for each center type, integrating the evaluation approach. The approach is validated in a case study in Munich, using real-life data. Simulation results analyze key performance indicators and provide recommendations for optimizing logistics and economic aspects in urban consolidation center planning. Efficient options include roll containers, electric pallet trucks, Last In – First Out storage, and gloves with integrated identification devices.**

Keywords – Cargo bikes; City logistics; Discrete-event simulation; Identification technologies; Urban consolidation centers.

I. Introduction

The volume of Courier, Express, and Parcel (CEP) shipments grew by 11.2 % to 4.51 billion shipments from 2011 to 2021. Annual growth of 4.7 % is expected up to 2026 [1]. Apart from extraordinary events, such as the COVID-19 pandemic, this is mainly due to changing consumer behavior, increasing urbanization, and growing demand for e-commerce products [2]. Online retail poses new challenges for urban delivery traffic, as more and more small shipments are to be delivered to customers more quickly [3]. To that end, city logistics is confronted with challenges similar to those industrial material flow systems are confronted with [4]. In addition to that, special services, such as same-day or same-hour delivery are gaining in importance [5]. Environmental protection measures and efficiency improvements are urgently needed. The concept of Urban Consolidation Centers (UCCs), which are located close to delivery areas, enables the distribution of goods flows and route-optimized delivery [3]. UCCs serve as transshipment points for environmentally friendly vehicles and as interfaces for alternative delivery concepts [6]. Simulation techniques help plan and optimize UCCs in neighborhoods with a relevant usage potential [7]. This article presents a simulation-based approach for the analysis of UCCs and the identification of feasible design premises.

The work is structured as follows: In Section II, the state of the art regarding design and operations of UCCs is presented and subsequently, research objectives are derived. In Section III, an approach for setting up simulation-based UCC analyses is presented and implemented with a case study example. Section IV concludes the work by summarizing the results and identifying limitations and potential future research work.

II. State of the Art and Research Objectives

A. *Urban consolidation centers for parcel distribution*

UCCs serve as transshipment hubs for high-volume shipments in densely populated areas, facilitating the flow of goods between shippers or recipients and regional distribution centers. Generally, transportation is provided by trucks in classes ranging from 3.5 to 12 tons.

Shipments are pre-sorted at regional distribution centers and typically consist of low-weight, low-volume goods delivered in high-density areas (see Figure 1). UCCs are supplied from CEP service providers' regional centers in the morning, using roll containers or pre-sorted boxes. UCCs can be either stationary or mobile, using pre-existing real estate or swap bodies/trailers to create temporary hubs. Mobile UCCs are transported to and from the established location by truck [8].

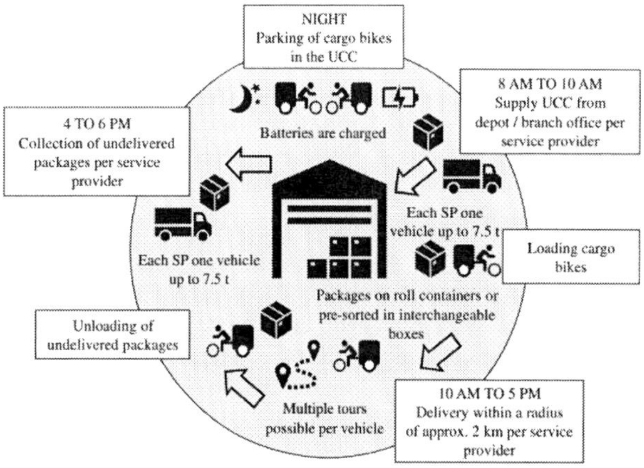

Figure 1. Operating scenario for a multi-user UCC, based on [8].

B. *Quantitative methods: discrete-event process simulation and methods-time measurement*

Discrete-Event Simulation (DES) examines event-driven process chains using multiple scenarios [9]. Transferring gained knowledge to the real-world system requires minimal differences between the initial system and the model [10]. System variants are compared and evaluated based on different criteria. This paper maps and models the material flow system in UCCs using DES, following five essential steps: Task analysis, model design, implementation, verification, validation, and application [11]. Methods-Time Measurement (MTM) determines standardized process times by breaking down human motion into steps [12]. It quantifies manual processes in UCCs, assisting in DES model parameterization by adding relevant partial times of basic movements to determine total activity time [13].

C. *Storage equipment: handling systems and identication technologies*

Two types of load carriers in UCCs are considered in this work: Roll containers and Euro pallets. Roll containers are self-driven with wheels, requiring no handling equipment. Euro pallets are handled using manually operated or electric pallet trucks [14]. Different identification technologies in warehouse logistics simplify package sorting and recognize package information [15]. They can be condensed to four representative main types of identification technologies, which are the following: Smartphone, glove with built-in scanning device (ID glove), stationary camera and RFID scanner. Cameras and RFID scanners require special workstations, while smartphones and ID gloves provide mobile solutions carried by workers during sorting, eliminating the necessity for separate workstations [16].

D. *Parcel sorting and storage operations*

Efficient storage systems prioritize fast access, short transport and walking distances and organized structures [17][18]. For UCCs, a row storage is the most common variant. It allows fast access and moderate investment costs. Thus, in the following, a row storage scheme is used for all configurations. Storage strategies aim to minimize distances, maximize capacity utilization, and prevent obsolescence. Besides First-In – First Out (FIFO) and Last In – First Out (LIFO), other strategies, such as optimizing service routes and combining orders, can be applied [16][19].

E. *Research objective*

The impact of UCCs on urban logistics has been studied in Barcelona (Spain) and Belo Horizonte (Brazil), considering economic and ecological factors [20][21]. Various methods have been developed to determine locations and identify factors affecting depot operations for enhanced collaboration among stakeholders [22][23][24][25]. Moreover, UCCs were evaluated for business opportunities and collaboration using Key Performance Indicators (KPIs) and DES models in a case study in Greece [26]. Also, the effectiveness of traditional delivery trucks and cargo bikes for parcel delivery was compared and assessed using the DES approach and agent- based simulation [27].

The previous research is strongly focused on the handling and delivery process and the general cooperative use of UCCs, examined from the macro perspective. The simulation-based investigation and evaluation of material flow and storage strategies, as well as their influence in combination with further configuration parameters within different UCC types is not considered accordingly. This results in two research objectives that this work addresses:

1) How can different UCC types be evaluated under variation of relevant layout parameters, as well as material flow and storage strategies by means of DES?

2) Which recommendations can be derived for the planning and dimensioning of UCCs, the processes to be carried out and the selection of identification technologies?

III. MODELING

In the following subsections it is explained how UCC operations are modeled using a DES approach, including the selection and implementation of different parameters.

A. *Concept of an evaluation approach*

The evaluation of UCCs requires defining relevant design parameters and assessment metrics that reflect realistic processes and can be integrated into simulation models for deriving meaningful conclusions. Prior to developing the DES model, all relevant parameters must be determined. They are the inputs and generate the system diversity by being set to different values in several combinations. MTM helps to quantify the them. The outputs are performance metrics, such as lead time and throughput, as well as monetary aspects, such as investments or personnel costs.

Table I summarizes all relevant design parameters based on the literature analysis. The UCC types studied include various container sizes, swap bodies (non-stackable freight containers specifically designed for road and rail transport), and storage rooms of different sizes (the small storage room having an area of 50 m² and the large one 100 m²). The parameters include four different combinations of parcel volume and weight (A, B, C, and D), subsequently referred to as parcel flow. Each one represents a distribution of parcel weight and volume. Flows with larger or heavier parcels yield a lower number of parcels in total. Standardized parcel formats are used. Volume and weight are calculated using average values. Roll containers and Euro pallets are used as load carriers, and respective volume utilization rates are determined. Also, various handling equipment for transporting the load carriers is considered. Identification technologies, such as barcode scanners and radio-frequency identification (RFID), and different storage strategies, such as FIFO, LIFO, and chaotic are used to capture parcel information and optimize the sorting and picking efficiency.

B. *Implementation with discrete-event process simulation*

In this subsection, the method for determining the number of required load carriers and calculating the capacities of UCCs for a certain application scenario is introduced. It is also explained how floor space utilization in warehouse management is determined.

TABLE I. MORPHOLOGICAL BOX CONTAINING THE IDENTIFIED DESIGN PARAMETERS AND THEIR CHARACTERISTICS.

Design Parameters	Characteristics of Design Parameters				
Parcel flow	A	B	C	D	
Load carrier	Roll container		Euro pallet		
Handling equipment	Manual operated pallet truck		Electric pallet truck		
Identification technology	Smartphone	ID glove	Camera	RFID	
Storage strategy	FIFO	LIFO	Chaotic		
UCC type	10 ft container	20 ft container	Swap body	Small storage room	Large storage room

To start, the number of required load carriers is determined based on the calculation of the load capacity of a single load carrier in terms of parcels. The load capacity depends on the assumed parcel volume in the respective use case, the internal volume of the respective load carrier, and the volume utilization rate the CEP provider is aiming for.

The internal volume V of a load carrier is determined using geometric dimensions from technical data for roll containers and Euro pallets. The load capacity C of a load carrier is calculated by multiplying V with the volume utilization rate ρ divided through the volume v of an individual parcel as

$$C = V \rho v^{-1}. \tag{1}$$

Hence, the number of load carriers can be computed as the number of parcels overall divided through the number of parcels a single load carrier can carry.

After that, suitable UCC types can be selected based on their storage capacities (see Figure 2 for an exemplary application with a 20 ft container, comparing the layout drawing and the simulation model). UCC types with storage capacities equal to or greater than the calculated number of load carriers are considered as potential solutions.

Figure 2 shows the simulation model with transport module (center), workstation module (upper left corner), and storage module (upper and lower part). The transport module consists of footpaths and workstations. The workstations define where the employee should stand during transfer or handling. The workstation module is composed of only two single stations. These are intended to simulate the process of placing the package on the table and the identification process by scanning it with a camera or RFID. Each cell of the warehouse module consists of a warehouse and two individual stations, and one cell is provided for each storage location. The warehouse allows to keep a single load carrier on it. Left and right single stations are used for depositing the load carrier during a temporary stopover and for transferring the parcels to the waiting load carrier in the UCC.

The floor space utilization rate is an important metric in warehouse management, representing the ratio of the space effectively utilized for operational purposes compared to the total warehouse area. A higher floor space utilization rate is generally desirable, but limits exist since warehouse operators and their equipment still need to move around. Floor space utilization rate is calculated using the ratio of used warehouse area and gross warehouse area.

Regarding the time analysis of the storage and retrieval, different time intervals are defined based on the sorting methods used. The total lead time is the sum of the time for storage executed by the truck driver and the time for retrieval (i.e., picking times) executed by the cargo bike rider. The process of retrieval begins with the cargo bike arriving at the UCC and ends when the last parcel assigned to the respective tour has been loaded into the bike. For all simulation runs, a medium-sized cargo bike with the loading capacity of 1.25 m^3 and a loading weight of 150 kg has been assumed.

In order to obtain a comprehensive understanding of the system behavior of a UCC, sufficient simulation results must be generated and collected. This can be accomplished by running multiple simulations. The execution of those simulation runs can be optimized using experimental design and thereby reducing the number of final runs and avoiding duplication. The simulation model, adapted to different UCC types, is created using suitable simulation software. It features an intuitive and modular user interface for easy implementation and parameter adaptability. Recorded simulation results are documented for subsequent data processing.

IV. CASE STUDY: APPLICATION IN MUNICH SCHWABING-WEST

This subsection presents an assessment approach for UCCs, discussing results and findings. A case study in Munich is used to compare different UCC types based on planning data. With the district of Schwabing-West as an example, the number of UCCs and parcel distribution are determined based on population size and delivery rates. Storage capacity and the number of carriers are taken into account to calculate the minimum number of UCCs required.

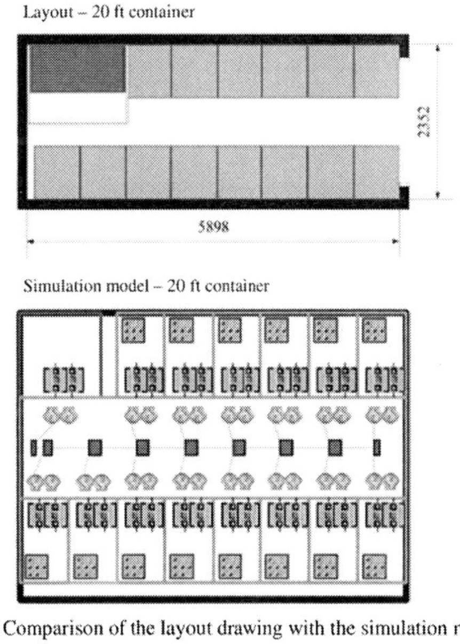

Figure 2. Comparison of the layout drawing with the simulation model of the 20 ft container.

In the example of Schwabing-West with 68204 inhabitants and an average delivery rate of 0.2 parcels per inhabitant and day, this results in a total volume of 13641 parcels per day [28][29]. There are five CEP service providers, each of which therefore has to process about 2730 parcels per day. Based on a UCC delivery radius of one kilometer, two UCC locations with a diameter of two kilometers are selected for sufficient coverage [30].

The estimated number of parcels per UCC that need to be processed on a daily basis is approximately 1,365. However, it should be noted that seasonal deviations of capacity demand can cause the necessity for a UCC to offer more storage capacities. The results presented in the following have been generated using an average over the four different parcel flow scenarios A to D and the respective simulation results. The number of UCCs in the district is kept as low as possible for as long as the capacity requirements are met.

With the assumption that only one type of UCC with the same parcel volumes exists in the planning area, a simulation model was developed to evaluate the processes within a UCC. The simulation model was generated with *Tecnomatix Plant Simulation* [31].

To vary the parameters in Table I, four test groups have been created. Test Group 1 (192 simulation runs) considered parcel flows and load carriers. In Group 2, handling devices were compared over 16 simulation runs. Group 3 was meant to compare identification technologies and storage strategies (320 runs). The scope of Group 4 with 18 simulation runs was the comparison of UCC layouts. This yields a total sum of 546 executed simulation runs.

The results were evaluated from a logistical and monetary point of view, considering setup and operational costs. In the following paragraphs, the results of this case study are presented. They are also shown in Figure 3.

At first, the choice of different load carriers is considered – see sub-figure 3(a). Throughput for storage and retrieval of roll containers and Euro pallets varies by the UCC type considered. Storage time per parcel tends to increase with a larger number of load carriers, as larger UCCs require longer transport and transit times. The cost comparison between roll containers and Euro pallets shows that Euro pallets have the lowest investment costs in most UCC type scenarios (since they are the less costly type of load carrier).

On the other hand, roll containers have lower average variable costs. Due to reduced operating times, the use of roll containers can reduce the total storage time significantly. The result is that the throughput for storage operations varies between roughly 2800 parcels per hour (p/h) for 10 ft containers and more than 9100 p/h in a large storage room when roll containers are used. The throughput that can be reached when using pallets varies between 2500 and 8400 p/h for the two respective UCC types. When it comes to retrieval, roll containers enable throughputs of 680 p/h for 10 ft containers and 370 p/h for large storage rooms, in contrast to 670 and 260 p/h for the pallets.

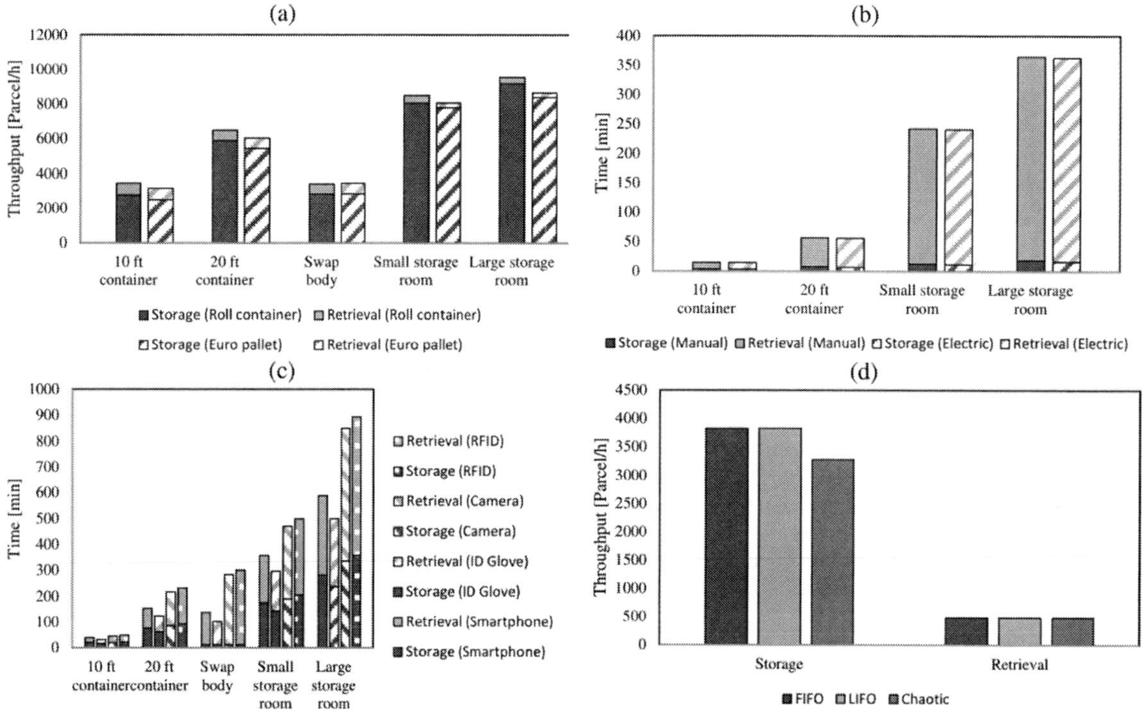

Figure 3. results of the case study simulation: (a) Throughput by storage and retrieval regarding load carriers (b) Storage and the retrieval time regarding handling devices (c) Storage and the retrieval time regarding identification technologies (d) Throughput regarding storage strategies for all UCCs.

Regarding floor space utilization, roll containers show a better utilization rate than pallets. Among the different layout types for UCCs, roll containers reach up to nine percentage points more in that metric. The reason for this can be found in the compact design. In a 20 ft container, the floor space utilization rate reaches the highest value of 38 %, whereas in the large storage room, only 12 % can be reached. This low floor space utilization is due to the layout structure of this large room which requires additional picking aisles, thereby reducing the amount of space available for storage purposes.

The next part of the case study is the examination of different handling devices – see sub-figure 3(b). Electric pallet trucks show a shorter storage time due to their better maneuverability and speed. This means that, when summing up the required lead time per parcel for storage and retrieval, electric pallet trucks can save less than one minute when a 10 ft container layout is used. However, with a large storage room, a lead time reduction of roughly 2.5 min can be observed. In relative figures, electric pallet trucks enable a lead time reduction between 0.7 % and 1.8 %. The retrieval time accounts for the largest share of the total lead time.

Hand pallet trucks, on the other hand, are more economical due to their lower purchase price. Depending on the type of UCC layout used (which means a different number of UCCs and therefore also a different number of handling devices are needed), the fixed costs can vary by a factor of 10. However, electric pallet trucks always cause about 260 % of the fixed costs of hand pallet trucks.

The next aspect covered by the case study are the different identification technologies for the parcel sorting – see sub-figure 3(c). The results show that the sorting speed of the different technologies is in descending order as follows: ID glove, smartphone, camera, and RFID scanner. The retrieval time accounts for a larger share of the total lead time compared to the storage time. The results show that the ID glove has the shortest total lead time for all UCC layout types, while stationary RFID scanning causes the longest lead time. The use of a smartphone as an identification device in parcel sorting is the most cost effective. The ID glove can reduce variable costs even more in most cases, but it is not always the most cost-effective solution overall due to its high purchase price. The use of cameras and RFID results in higher capital costs and lower storage performance.

The final subject considered in the case study is the influence of different storage strategies – see sub-figure 3(d). Regarding storage time based on the average value of all the UCCs, the chaotic storage principle achieves the largest storage time and thus the lowest efficiency due to the additional documentation the operator needs to deal with. The FIFO and LIFO principles, on the other hand, have a lower storage time and therefore a higher throughput (both reaching 17 % higher values than chaotic storage). For retrieval, the storage strategies perform similarly to each other, and the achieved throughputs vary by less than 1 %. As a result, the chaotic storage can be observed to have the highest personnel costs among the three storage strategies.

Overall, the results show that the use of roll containers, electric pallet trucks, ID glove and the LIFO storage principle are the most efficient design options.

V. Discussion

A. *Research findings*

In this paper, UCCs as important parts of inner-city distribution logistics were evaluated using DES and varying different design parameters. As a starting point, the relevant design parameters and different types of UCCs were determined. These parameters were then summarized according to study objectives, used for an evaluation approach, and implemented in simulation models. Those DES models were adapted for all UCC types considered.

In the planning example for Munich Schwabing-West, several scenarios for parcel quantities, sizes, and weights were assigned to various UCC types. The optimal number of UCCs to deal with these parcel volumes was then determined. Subsequently, the different UCC types were evaluated and compared using the evaluation approach and the constructed simulation model. To evaluate the different UCCs, logistical and monetary aspects were considered. The cost analysis focused only on acquisition and personnel costs but could be extended in the future to include insurance and ancillary costs, such as electricity and water.

Through the sensible use of identification and communication technologies and electric devices, logistical performance in the UCC could be significantly increased, while personnel costs could be lowered through the reduction of working time. This reduction could be reached by the increased identification efficiency in parcel sorting related to the use of reliability-enhancing identification technologies. However, due to the high purchase price, introducing technological equipment is not necessarily an absolute ideal solution for all UCC scenarios. Furthermore, it should be noted that the choice of the appropriate load carrier depends on the specific requirements of the UCC and the nature of the storage and delivery processes.

In the last part of this work, the recommendations for the design parameters of UCCs were derived regarding the simulation results and the applied evaluation criteria. The evaluation approach developed for this purpose and the designed and built simulation model were thus verified and validated on the basis of the quantitative simulation results from the practical case study in Munich Schwabing-West.

B. *Limitations and future work*

However, the simulation runs executed for the evaluation were reduced to only that amount which was necessary for the most relevant study objectives in order to save computational time and modeling effort. It could lead to the risk that resulting simulation results are not taking into account potential hidden interactions between certain design parameters in combination with the UCC types.

The time window per day for the employee was consequently set to eight hours. However, this working time might not be optimal for all potential use cases. Also, the warehouse process was only simulated for one UCC within one day. In the future, the simulation model could be extended to several UCCs with a longer time interval, e.g., one week, in order to provide more accurate results about the cooperation between the UCC and CEP service providers.

The investigation of the UCC system can be further optimized in subsequent research through test trials in real laboratories in order to gain a comprehensive overview of UCCs in various application scenarios and to ensure the most precise and comprehensive evaluation possible.

VI. Conclusion and Future Work

With the use and expansion of environmentally friendly delivery transport, such as electric cargo bikes, and the high handling capacity performed in inner-city areas, UCCs become an increasingly important and conceivable solution to make the last mile delivery of CEP service more efficient. By using UCCs and working closely with cities and municipalities, logistics and traffic, problems can be mitigated to help reduce congestion and emissions in inner-city residential areas. The consideration of costs involved depending on the choice of configuration parameters helps to select an appropriately designed UCC. To this end, the use of roll containers, or (alternatively) electric pallet trucks combined with ID gloves helps in finding a balance between costs and achieved logistics performance.

References

[1] BIEK, CEP Study 2022: A market analysis in Germany, 2022. [Online]. Available: https://www.biek.de/publikationen/studien.html (retrieved: October 2023)

[2] IHK, Micro depots in connected cities: a study on Krefeld, Mönchengladbach and Neuss, 2019.

[3] K. Havers, Guidelines for the sustainable design of urban delivery traffic systems, 2021. [Online]. Available: https://digital.zlb.de/viewer/metadata/34654392/0/ (retrieved: October 2023)

[4] M. Wuennenberg, P. Vollmuth, J. Xu, J. Fottner, and B. Vogel-Heuser, "Transformability in Material Flow Systems: Towards an Improved Product Development Process," in Lecture Notes in Networks and Systems, Managing and Implementing the Digital Transformation, 2022, pp. 3–14. DOI: 10.1007/978-3-031-14317-5_1

[5] P. H. Voß, Logistics - an underestimated industry of the future: Strategies and solutions along Supply Chain 4.0, 2019. [Online]. Available: https://link.springer.com/content/pdf/10.1007/978-3-658-27317-0.pdf (retrieved: October 2023)

[6] E. Taniguchi and R. van der Heijden, "An evaluation methodology for city logistics. in: Transport logistics," Classics in Transport Analysis, no. 5, 2002, pp. 65–90.

[7] W. Hofmann, T. Assmann, P. Neghabadi, V. Cung, and J. Tolujevs, Eds., A simulation tool to assess the integration of cargo bikes into an urban distribution system, 2017.

[8] IHK, Micro depots in connected cities: a study on Krefeld, Mönchengladbach and Neuss, 2021.

[9] Simulation of logistics, material flow, and production systems, 3633, Verein Deutscher Ingenieure.

[10] K. Gutenschwager, M. Rabe, S. Spieckermann, and S. Wenzel, Simulation in production and logistics. Berlin, Heidelberg: Springer Vieweg, 2017.

[11] J. Banks, D. Gerstein, and S. Searles, Modeling processes, validation, and verification of complex simulations: A survey. Methodology and validation, 1988.

[12] H.-J. Bullinger, Guidelines for a personnel-oriented design of competitive work stations: Springer-Verlag, 2013.

[13] M. Wuennenberg, B. Wegerich, and J. Fottner, "Optimization of Internal Logistics using a combined BPMN and Simulation Approach," in Proceedings of the 36th ECMS International Conference on Modelling and Simulation ECMS 2022, Ålesund, Norway, 2022, pp. 13–19.

[14] H. Martin, Transportation and storage logistics: Springer-Verlag, 2016.

[15] M. Kärkkäinen and J. Holmström, "Wireless product identification: enabler for handling efficiency, customisation and information sharing," Supply chain management: an International journal, vol. 7, no. 4, pp. 242–252, 2002.

[16] H. Martin, Storage logistics, transportation planning, and controlling of intralogistics systems: Springer Vieweg Wiesbaden, 2014.

[17] D. Arnold, H. Isermann, A. Kuhn, H. Tempelmeier, and K. Furmans, Handbook for logistics: Springer, 2008.

[18] T. Schmidt, Ed., Internal logistics. Berlin, Heidelberg: Springer Vieweg, 2019.

[19] H. Gleißner and J. Femerling, "Fundamentals in logistics," in Logistik: Gabler, 2008, pp. 3–20. [Online]. Available: https://link.springer.com/chapter/10.1007/978-3-8349-9547-6_2 (retrieved: October 2023)

[20] M. Roca-Riu and M. Estrada, "An evaluation of urban consolidation centers through logistics systems analysis in circumstances where companies have equal market shares," Procedia-Social and Behavioral Sciences, vol. 39, pp. 796–806, 2012.

[21] V. Correia, L. Oliveira, and A. Guerra, "Economical and environmental analysis of an urban consolidation center for Belo Horizonte City (Brazil)," Procedia-Social and Behavioral Sciences, vol. 39, pp. 770–782, 2012.

[22] G. Battaia, L. Faure, G. Marqués, R. Guillaume, and J. R. Montoya-Torres, Eds., A methodology to anticipate the activity level of collaborative networks: The case of urban consolidation: Taylor & Francis, 2014.

[23] A. Anderluh, v. Hemmelmayr, and D. Rüdiger, "Analytic hierarchy process for city hub location selection-The Viennese case," Transportation Research Procedia, vol. 46, pp. 77–84, 2020.

[24] R. Dupas, J. Deschamps, E. Taniguchi, A. Qureshi, and T. Hsu, "Optimizing the location selection of urban consolidation centers with sustainability considerations in the city of Bordeaux," Research in Transportation Business & Management, p. 100943, 2023.

[25] M. Savall-Manyó and I. Ribas, "Location of micro-urban consolidation centres for the superblocks in Barcelona," IFAC-PapersOnLine, vol. 55, no. 10, pp. 145–150, 2022.

[26] M. Rabe, A. Klueter, and A. Wuttke, Eds., Evaluating the consolidation of distribution flows using a discrete event supply chain simulation tool: Application to a case study in Greece: IEEE, 2018.

[27] A. Ballano, A. Al-Rahamneh, A. Serrano-Hernandez, and J. Faulin, "Agent-based modelling and simulation for hub and electric last mile distribution in Vienna," Procedia Computer Science, vol. 220, pp. 718–723, 2023.

[28] BIEK – A study on parcel occurence in German cities. [Online]. Available: https://www.biek.de/presse/meldung/die-meisten-pakete-pro-einwohner-gibts-in-m%C3%BCnchen-stuttgart-und-d%C3%BCsseldorf.html (retrieved: October 2023).

[29] Statista, Inhabitants of the Munich districts in 2022. [Online]. Available: https://de.statista.com/statistik/daten/studie/1106611/umfrage/einwohnerzahl-der-stadtbezirke-von-muenchen/ (retrieved: October 2023).

[30] BIEK, "Micro Depots - An advantage for cities," 2019.

[31] Tecnomatix Plant Simulation Software. [Online]. Available: https://plm.sw.siemens.com/de-DE/tecnomatix/products/plant-simulation-software/ (retrieved: October 2023).

Qualitative Simulation of Causal Dynamics in Higher Education using Fuzzy Cognitive Maps

Levent Yilmaz
Department of Computer Science and Software Engineering
Auburn University
Auburn, AL
email: yilmaz@auburn.edu

***Abstract*—Universities are complex organizations that are comprised of semi-autonomous interacting units that adapt to evolving demands and regulations. Administrative decision-making requires viewing a university as an adaptive system with a complex causal network of interactions. This paper presents a qualitative causal simulation model based on the Fuzzy Cognitive Map (FCM) formalism to demonstrate exploratory cause-effect analysis of resource tensions and quality in public higher education institutes. The model is focused on a selected subset of factors with the primary aim of demonstrating the use of FCM to support model-centric thinking. The FCM formalism is simulated under a factorial experiment design that examines the interaction among state funding, teaching capacity, and research capacity.**

***Index Terms*—qualitative simulation; fuzzy cognitive map; higher education; complexity**

I. INTRODUCTION

According to the Education Data Initiative [1], as of July 2022, 73.0% of college students at all levels attend public institutions. Policies aimed at these institutions have a significant influence on higher education. In recent years, increasing fiscal challenges in the public higher education environment resulted in the development of new administrative models that emphasize the ability to generate income to provide additional revenue. Among such capabilities are sponsored research activities based on contracts and patents. Such activities promoted an environment that can sustain fundable research with implications on hiring policies and incentives for promotion and balance teaching load with increasing research commitments.

Increasing fiscal tensions in state funding of public higher education impact the quality of education, graduation rates, and overall organizational performance of universities [2]. Factors that influence organizational performance can be classified into separate activity and policy categories, such as state funding, affordability, target population characteristics, faculty teaching and research load, compensation, and admission. These separate activity zones interact through complex mechanisms, making it challenging to predict the outcomes of decisions and emergent behavior due to positive and negative feedback loops among factors.

Improving graduation rates, research funding, and overall system quality can involve exploring various options, including staff compensation, faculty incentives for productive participation, teaching and research loads, hybrid instruction, and improving access and affordability to the target population. In this paper, the systems approach with an exploratory modeling and analysis strategy is advocated to provide a foundation to demonstrate policy analysis in the context of higher education. The proposed model is focused on a selected subset of factors with the primary objective of demonstrating the use of the computational Fuzzy Cognitive Map (FCM) [3] formalism to support model-centric thinking.

The rest of the paper is structured as follows. In section 2, background on simulation methodologies used in the simulation of university dynamics is reviewed. FCM formalism is introduced in section 3 to specify the fundamental principles of FCMs and the dynamics of the FCM model. Section 4 presents the implementation and preliminary experiments with the model, as well as a sensitivity analysis of the dynamics to discern cause-effect relations under hypothetical scenarios. Section 5 concludes with a summary of the findings and limitations of the model.

II. BACKGROUND

Computational models are effective tools in evaluating organizational dynamics to assess the effectiveness of policies in the presence of a multitude of interacting factors. Simulation modeling can help explore the effectiveness of university operations in achieving organizational outcomes while providing a predictive and prescriptive tool for policy evaluation. The use of computational models in education has a rich history. Although the use of qualitative simulations of higher education with FCM models remains to be explored, both Agent-based Modeling (ABM) [4] and system dynamics models [5] [6] are widely used. Next, we provide a brief review of selected ABM and System Dynamics (SD) approaches, followed by a discussion on how the FCM formalism, which is the focus of this paper, can complement the ABM and the SD perspectives.

A. Agent-Based Modeling

Agent-based modeling is a methodology for developing computational models of systems in terms of autonomous agents to simulate the decisions, actions, and interactions of discrete entities. Such entities can represent a broad range of system elements, from individual humans to collectives, such as organizations and communities. Agent-based simulation models examine a broad range of aspects of the higher education system and its interactions with the broader context.

In [7], an agent-based model of a public university is developed to study the impact of various organizational decisions on institutional performance with a specific focus on the financial perspective. During the Covid pandemic, universities faced significant challenges in avoiding the spread of outbreaks on campus [8]. Computational studies of randomized testing, contact tracing, and quarantining reveal the effectiveness of alternative strategies in protecting students, faculty, and staff [9]. Simulation models of innovation dynamics explore industry-university links to examine the impact of collaboration structures on innovation effectiveness [10].

Simulation models grounded in theory facilitate understanding system behavior if the real-world behavior unfolds consistently with the premises of the respective theory. For example, in [11], social impact theory tests social communication and resource allocation on STEM yield. Besides education systems, agent-based models are used to study scientific activity and clustering of research activity into scientific domains and disciplines [12]. Similarly, [13] uses a simulation model to represent scientific activity as a sociopolitical system.

B. System Dynamics

System Dynamics (SD) modeling [5] is a mathematical modeling approach to represent systems and their continuous non-linear behavior over time. SD models are used to explain and predict the dynamics of complex issues and problems ranging from artificial to social and natural systems.

System dynamics modeling in higher education has a long history with a broad range of applications overviewed by an early taxonomy of SD models in higher education [14]. Relatively recent research in this area involves capacity planning and policy evaluation. In [15], the implementation of sustainable development education programs is examined with a focus on the sustainability competencies of students. As a decision support tool, system dynamics models contribute to exploring efficient resource management and capacity planning for academic programs [16] [17].

Alternative simulation formalisms, including semi-quantitative and highly interpretable causal simulation formalisms, such as FCM, can also offer avenues to perform thought experiments before developing detailed high-resolution models.

C. Fuzzy Cognitive Maps

FCMs model feedback causal relations in webs of causality and system design/policy/strategy variables [3]. FCM formalism combines neural network theory and fuzzy logic [18] synergistically. FCMs are fuzzy signed directed graphs that allow degrees of causal influence and event occurrence. Such causal models can simulate a wide range of system designs, scenarios, and decision processes. Their nonlinear dynamics permit forward-chaining inference from input causes and design options to output effects. Users can directly add detailed dynamics and feedback links to the causal model or infer them with statistical learning laws [19]. Users can fuse or combine FCMs from multiple experts by weighting and adding the underlying fuzzy edge matrices recursively if needed.

III. Foundations of the Fuzzy Cognitive Map Formalism

An FCM concept node is fuzzy because it can take values in the unit interval [0,1]. Therefore, its values over time define a fuzzy set. This implies that a concept node that describes a property or system state both occurs and does not occur to some degree at the same time. A simple FCM consists of n concept nodes C_j and n^2 directed fuzzy causal edges e_{ij}. The concept nodes $C_1, C_2, \ldots, C_n$ are nonlinear and represent variable concepts or factors in a causal system. The activation value of a concept node $C_i(t_k)$ measures the degree to which the concept C_i occurs in the causal dynamics at time t_k. The FCM state vector $\mathrm{C}(t_k)$ provides a snapshot of the FCM system at time t_k. In addition to the non-linear dynamics of the concept nodes, an FCM model must also specify the n^2 directed and signed causal edge values e_{ij}.

The activation value of the concept j is determined at time t_k on the scalar input $x_j(t_k)$ that reaches and aggregates all the causal activation inflowing to C_j. A non-linear function Φ_j converts $x_j(t_k)$ into the concept's new state $C_j(t_{k+1})$.

$$C_j(t_{k+1}) = \Phi_j(\sum_{i=1}^{n} C_i(t_k)\, e_{ij}(t_k) + I_j(t_k))$$

where $I_j(t_k)$ is an external input at time t_k. The simplest threshold function is a hard threshold that produces bivalent, on-off concept node values:

$$C_j(t_{k+1}) = \begin{cases} 0 & if \sum_{i=1}^{n} C_i(t_k)\, e_{ij}(t_k) + I_j(t_k) \leq 0 \\ 1 & if \sum_{i=1}^{n} C_i(t_k)\, e_{ij}(t_k) + I_j(t_k) > 0 \end{cases}$$

The external input can be set to high (or low) values to ensure that a concept is always on (or off). By fixing the activation value of a node, specific strategy configurations can be tested. A monotonic increasing Φ_j nonlinear function can be used for a continuous dynamic system. Logistic causal activation functions have a sigmoidal structure that approximates the hard threshold function if the shape parameter $c > 0$ is large enough:

$$C_j(t_{k+1}) = \frac{1}{1 + exp(-c\sum_{i=1}^{n} C_i(t_k)\, e_{ij}(t_k) - cI_j(t_k))}$$

Alternative approaches to modeling causal worlds are System Dynamics (SD) models [20] and Bayesian Belief networks (BBNs) [21]. System-dynamics models facilitate representing and simulating causal interactions. Domain experts or random experiments often choose static parameters of the subsystems and their interconnections. On the other hand, FCMs allow data-driven adaptation of the model structure and parameters.

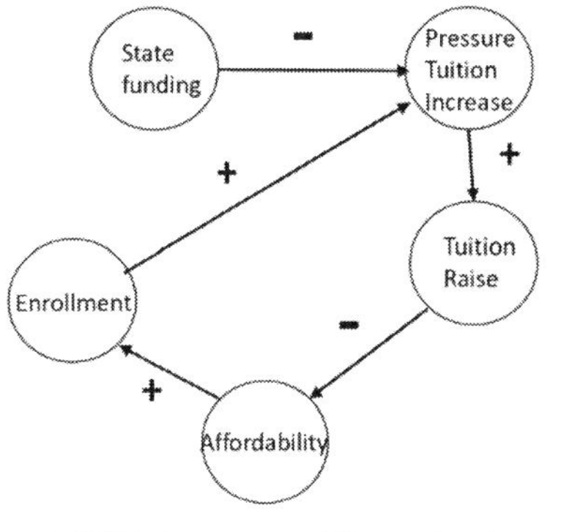

(a) FCM Concepts and Dependencies

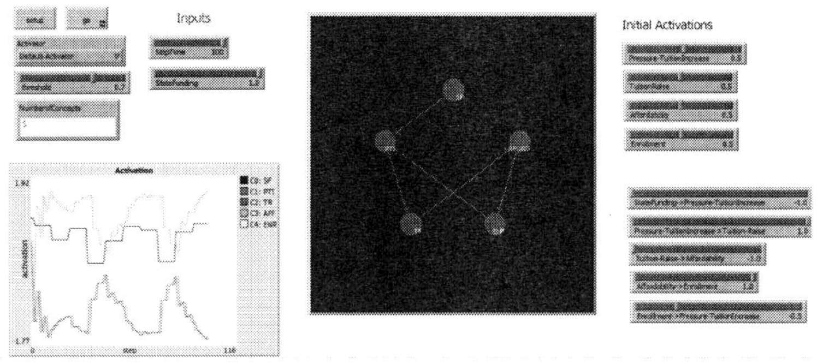

(b) Netlogo Implementation of the FCM Model

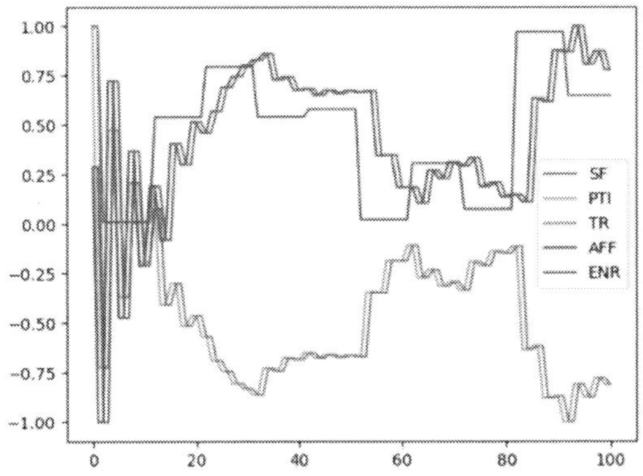

(c) Normalized Activation Levels

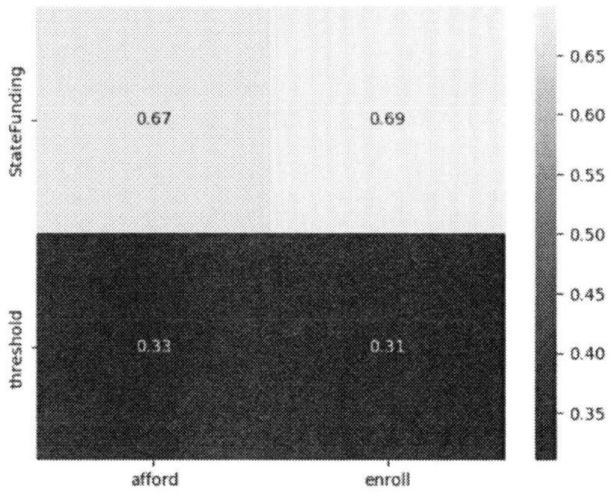

(d) Feature Scoring

Fig. 1: Face Validity of the FCM Implementation

Statistical learning algorithms estimate causal edges from training data. Experts can also state edge values directly. While SD models include stochastic behavior through sensitivity analyses at the end of modeling, FCMs build uncertainty into the causal structure.

BBNs model uncertain causal worlds with conditional probabilities that require using a known joint probability distribution over all the nodes of the directed graph. This may not be practical for a large number of nodes. Forward inference on a BBN also tends to be computationally intensive. Furthermore, the directed graph is usually acyclic and thus has no closed loops. The acyclic structure simplifies the probability structure but ignores the feedback of the causal units.

IV. A Qualitative Simulation Model of University Activity Dynamics

To illustrate the utility of qualitative simulation of university activities via a Fuzzy Cognitive Map, we start our analysis with a baseline model with minimal features. The baseline model is intended to assess the accuracy and face validity of implementing FCM in the NetLogo environment [22]. Figure 1a presents five concepts and their relations.

The *State Funding* is the input concept that is varied to assess the impact of fiscal tensions on the affordability and enrollment levels. According to [23], the decrease in state funding levels increases *pressure for a tuition increase*, which then results in an increased likelihood of *tuition increase*. These relations are specified as qualitative positive and negative dependencies. The extent of the impact of tuition increases on the affordability of higher education is well documented. Using the empirical findings reported in [24], the FCM model shown in Figure 1a introduces a negative relation between tuition raise and affordability. Furthermore, according to [25], decreasing affordability reduces enrollment levels. In relation to the dependency between enrollment levels and pressure for tuition increase, we consider the empirical results that suggest diseconomies of scale for large universities [26]. Finally, the causal link between enrollment and tuition closes the feedback loop.

The conceptual model is implemented within the NetLogo environment shown in Figure 1b. The Netlogo model is available at *github.com/yilmale/University*. In the implementation, the values of the weights of causal dependencies between variables are set to 1.0 for positive causal relations and -1.0 for negative relations. The *StateFunding* variable is updated episodically every 10 time steps and kept constant during each interval to validate the expected trends in the activation levels of enrollment and affordability. As shown in Figure 1c, the increase (decrease) in affordability and enrollment follows with a slight lag the increase (decrease) in the state funding level. Similarly, the change in the activation of pressure for tuition raise and the tuition rate follows the change in the state funding activation in the expected direction. Feature scoring analysis of simulation data, shown in Figure 1d, reveals the significance of the *state funding* variable on affordability and enrollment levels. The minimal baseline model facilitates instilling confidence in implementing the interactive activation dynamics process underlying the FCM formalism.

The model is extended with additional concepts representing the student-faculty ratio, student retention, graduation rate, and quality of experience. In the absence of new faculty hiring and everything else being equal, an increase in enrollment levels results in an increase in student-faculty ratio, negatively influencing student retention. Lower levels of student retention are expected to reduce graduation rates. Furthermore, higher levels of student-faculty ratio adversely affect experience quality, which is an important criterion for increasing graduation rates. The minimal FCM, shown in Figure 1a, is extended in Figure 2 to explore the impact of *State Funding* on *Graduation Rate* under the hypothetical frame characterized by the selected concepts and conjectured dependencies.

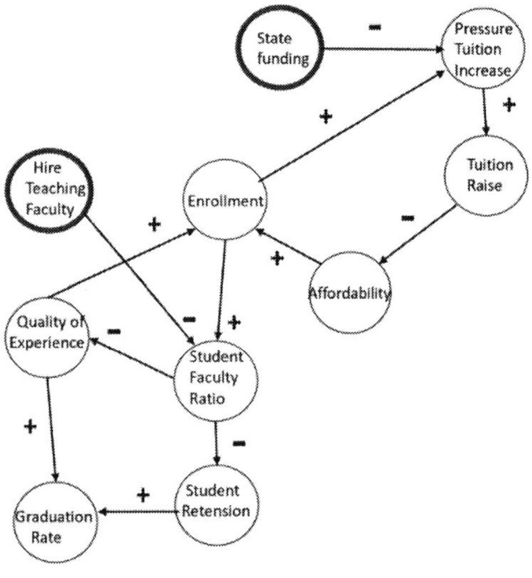

Fig. 2: Extended FCM Model.

Simulation of the FCM with the extended model reveals in Figure 3 that graduation rates decline regardless of state funding activity in the absence of teaching faculty hiring activity.

The factorial experiment examining the interaction between state funding and hiring teaching faculty shows that hiring teaching faculty is critical to increasing graduation rate activity. State funding does not produce sufficient graduation activity at lower teaching support levels, assuming that state funding does not contribute to reducing the student-faculty ratio through other mechanisms. The heatmap shown in Figure 4, in the absence of other factors, illustrates the significance

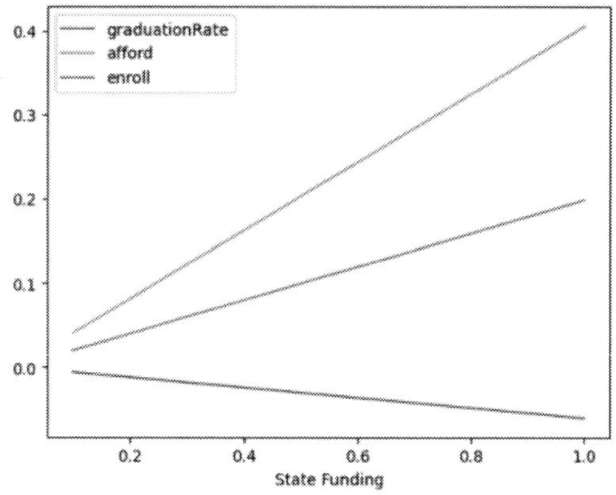

Fig. 3: Impact of State Funding on Graduation Rate in the Absence of Teaching Faculty

of teaching faculty on the graduation rate.

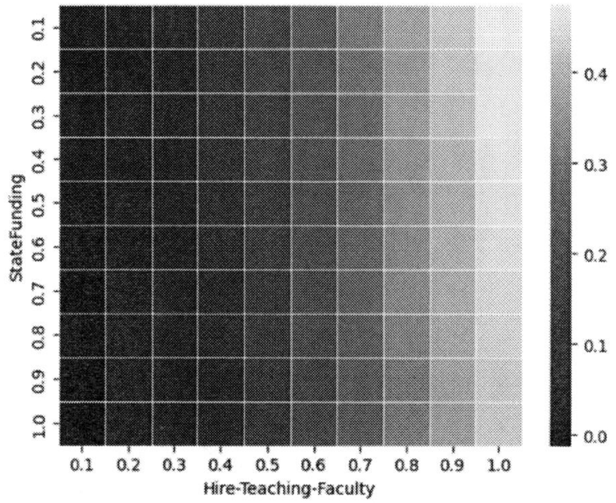

Fig. 4: Impact of State Funding and Teaching Faculty on Graduation Rate

To examine the role of the research component of a university, we extend the model to include additional concepts and dependencies involving sponsored research. However, exploring research activities and their impact on the quality of experience and graduation rates are limited to the current framework shown in Figure 5. In the extended model, for illustration purposes, *Hiring-Research-Faculty* is considered as an input concept that can be controlled by the university administration. By hiring research faculty, the university can be expected to increase the level of *Sponsored Research*, which generates new *Revenue*. Additional resources generated by sponsored research offices through indirect cost recovery mechanisms, as well as patents and innovations, stemming from the increased research activity, lower the pressure for tuition increase.

Sponsored research is expected to increase the research activity by faculty specified by the Faculty-Research node in the

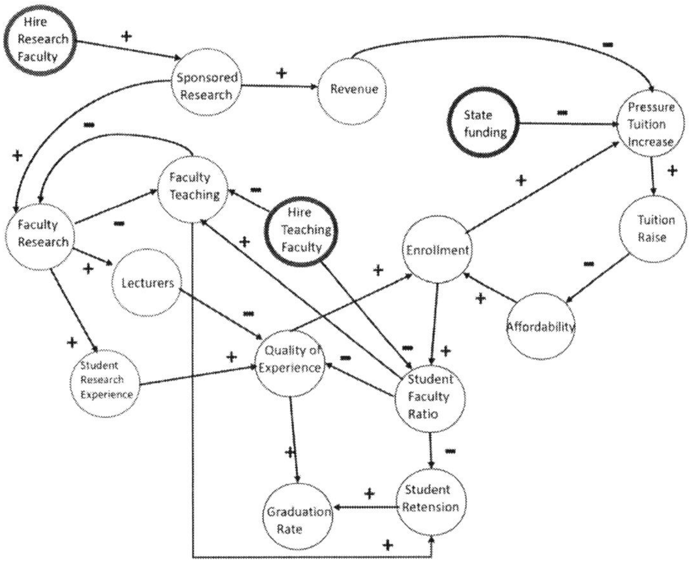

Fig. 5: Extending the FCM Model with Activities in the Research Zone

FCM. However, more faculty research results in lower levels of teaching activity due to administrative policies such as course buyouts or assigning teaching responsibilities to graduate students or lecturers. Delegation of teaching to lecturers reduces the quality of experience for students, resulting in an adverse impact on graduation and student retention. On the other hand, with increased faculty research activity, students have more opportunities to be involved in research, and such research experience contributes to an increased quality of experience. These conjectured causal dependencies are conceptualized in the FCM model shown in Figure 5.

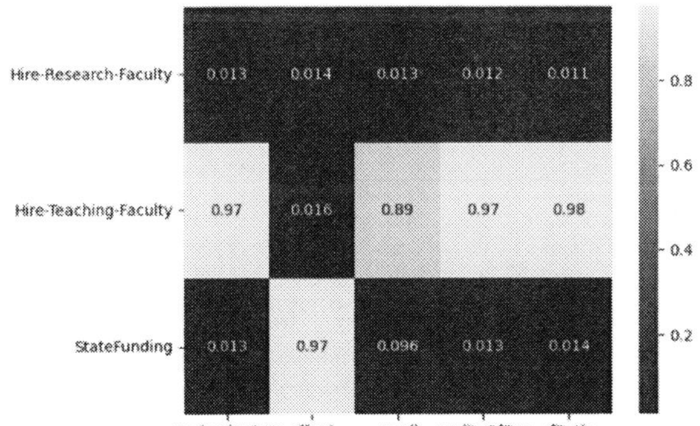

Fig. 6: Feature Analysis of the Extended Analysis

The simulation of the extended FCM explores the tension among state funding, research faculty hiring, and teaching faculty hiring. The model does not make resource allocation decisions among research and teaching activities. Instead, at a given level of state funding, and given the causal relations shown in Figure 5, the teaching faculty factor significantly impacts all outputs except *affordability*. On the other hand, as shown in Figure 6, state funding affects affordability, and the research component does not have significance on output metrics under the causal constraints of the model. Regarding the availability of teaching resources, the graduation rate declines with small levels of teaching faculty capacity. As shown in Figure 7a, increasing the teaching resource capacity beyond the inflection point consistently improves the graduation rate performance.

On the other hand, an increase in the research capacity improves the graduation rate through moderate levels of increase in student research experience that positively affects overall student experience. However, increasing the research load over the inflection point decreases the overall student experience and graduation rate due to its impact on suppressing teaching capacity. Figure 7b shows the observed behavioral trend.

The detailed ANOVA analysis, shown in Figure 8, of the quality of experience outcome supports the Feature Scoring analysis by highlighting the significance of state funding and teaching capacity. Two-way interactions between the factors reveal that the impact of individual factors is not dependent on other factors.

V. CONCLUSIONS

Analyzing policies in the higher education system requires understanding nonlinear dependencies between factors, including positive and negative feedback loops that can lead to nontrivial outcomes. For such complex systems, the tools and models of complexity can offer reliable frameworks to gain insight into the causal dynamics of constituent elements. In this paper, we demonstrated a semi-qualitative model based on the Fuzzy Cognitive Map formalism and conducted experiments to examine the tension among state funding, research capacity, and teaching capacity in relation to the quality of student experience and graduation rates. The causal dependencies

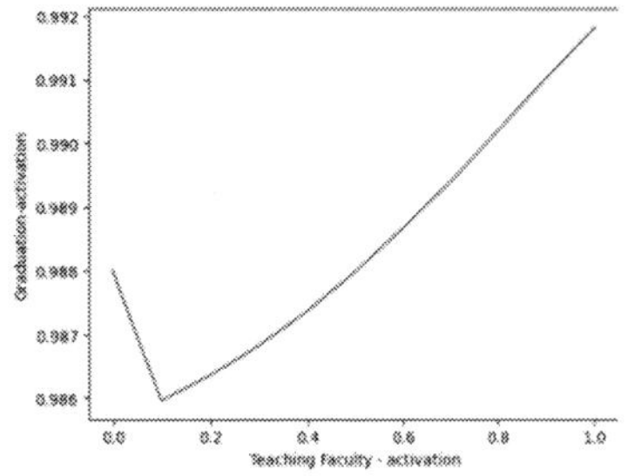

(a) The Impact of Teaching Capacity on Graduation Rate

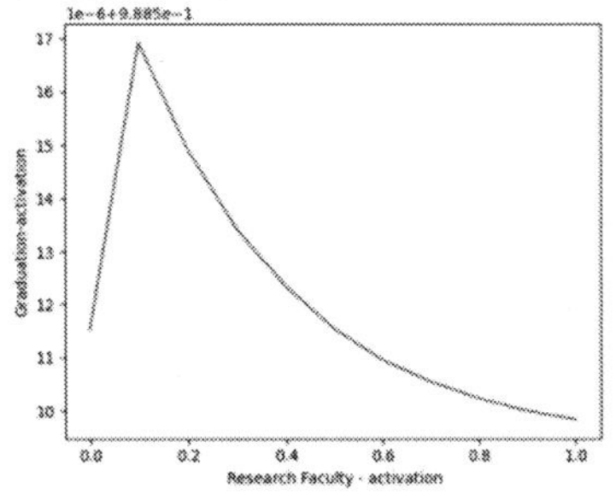

(b) The Impact of Research Capacity on Graduation Rate

Fig. 7: Impact of Teaching and Research Capacity on Graduation Rate

q: Quality of Experience, S: State Funding, T: Teaching Faculty, R: Research Faculty

Dep. Variable:	q	R-squared:	0.815
Model:	OLS	Adj. R-squared:	0.814
Method:	Least Squares	F-statistic:	970.7
		Prob (F-statistic):	0.00
		Log-Likelihood:	2956.4
No. Observations:	1331	AIC:	-5899.
Df Residuals:	1324	BIC:	-5862.
Df Model:	6		
Covariance Type:	nonrobust		

	coef	std err	t	P>|t|	[0.025	0.975]
Intercept	0.2839	0.004	75.393	0.000	0.277	0.291
S	0.0055	0.006	0.987	0.324	-0.005	0.016
T	0.1728	0.006	30.922	0.000	0.162	0.184
R	-0.0001	0.006	-0.027	0.979	-0.011	0.011
T:R	-6.101e-05	0.007	-0.008	0.993	-0.014	0.014
S:R	1.571e-05	0.007	0.002	0.998	-0.014	0.014
S:T	0.0024	0.007	0.335	0.737	-0.012	0.017

Omnibus:	304.477	Durbin-Watson:	0.093
Prob(Omnibus):	0.000	Jarque-Bera (JB):	543.789
Skew:	1.463	Prob(JB):	8.27e-119
Kurtosis:	4.116	Cond. No.	21.5

Fig. 8: ANOVA Analysis

presented in the model are based on theoretical and empirical findings reported in the extant literature. The results indicate the significance of teaching capacity on graduation rates, while state funding affects the affordability of higher education.

REFERENCES

[1] EDI, "College enrollment student demographic statistics," 2022, retrieved: September, 2023. [Online]. Available: https://educationdata.org/college-enrollment-statistics

[2] G. Lucianelli and F. Citro, "Financial conditions and financial sustainability financial financial sustainability in higher education: A literature review," *Financial sustainability in public administration: Exploring the concept of financial health*, pp. 23–53, 2017.

[3] O. Osoba and B. Kosko, "Beyond dags: modeling causal feedback with fuzzy cognitive maps," *arXiv preprint arXiv:1906.11247*, 2019.

[4] E. Bonabeau, "Agent-based modeling: Methods and techniques for simulating human systems," *Proceedings of the national academy of sciences*, vol. 99, no. suppl_3, pp. 7280–7287, 2002.

[5] J. W. Forrester, "System dynamics and the lessons of 35 years," *A systems-based approach to policymaking*, pp. 199–240, 1993.

[6] B. K. Bala, F. M. Arshad, and K. M. Noh, *System Dynamics: Modelling and Simulation*. Springer, 2017.

[7] P. J. Roebber and G. R. Meadows, "Simulating alternative approaches to addressing fiscal resource tensions and quality in us public higher education," *Journal of Education Finance*, pp. 81–108, 2012.

[8] J. Tang, S. Vinayavekhin, M. Weeramongkolkul, C. Suksanon, K. Pattarapremcharoen, S. Thiwathittayanuphap, and N. Leelawat, "Agent-based simulation and modeling of covid-19 pandemic: a bibliometric analysis," *Journal of Disaster Research*, vol. 17, no. 1, pp. 93–102, 2022.

[9] P. T. Gressman and J. R. Peck, "Simulating covid-19 in a university environment," *Mathematical biosciences*, vol. 328, p. 108436, 2020.

[10] P. Ahrweiler, A. Pyka, and N. Gilbert, "A new model for university-industry links in knowledge-based economies," *Journal of Product Innovation Management*, vol. 28, no. 2, pp. 218–235, 2011.

[11] T. T. Allen and N. Davis, "A simple agent-based social impact theory model of student stem selection," in *Proceedings of the 2010 Winter Simulation Conference*. IEEE, 2010, pp. 278–289.

[12] N. Gilbert, "A simulation of the structure of academic science," *Sociological research online*, vol. 2, no. 2, pp. 91–105, 1997.

[13] M. Mölders, R. D. Fink, and J. Weyer, "Modeling scientists as agents. how scientists cope with the challenges of the new public management of science," *Journal of Artificial Societies and Social Simulation*, vol. 14, no. 4, p. 6, 2011.

[14] M. Kennedy, "Towards a taxonomy of system dynamics models of higher education," in *Proceedings of the 18th International Conference of the System Dynamics Society (2000) 6-10 August 2000 Bergen, Norway*, 2000, pp. 1–12.

[15] E. Faham, A. Rezvanfar, S. H. M. Mohammadi, and M. R. Nohooji, "Using system dynamics to develop education for sustainable development in higher education with the emphasis on the sustainability competencies of students," *Technological Forecasting and Social Change*, vol. 123, pp. 307–326, 2017.

[16] S. M. Dahlan and N. Yahaya, "A system dynamics model for determining educational capacity of higher education institutions," in *2010 Second International Conference on Computational Intelligence, Modelling and Simulation*. IEEE, 2010, pp. 285–290.

[17] L. M. Strauss and D. Borenstein, "A system dynamics model for long-term planning of the undergraduate education in brazil," *Higher Education*, vol. 69, pp. 375–397, 2015.

[18] E. I. Papageorgiou, "Review study on fuzzy cognitive maps and their applications during the last decade," in *2011 IEEE international conference on fuzzy systems (FUZZ-IEEE 2011)*. IEEE, 2011, pp. 828–835.

[19] J. L. Salmeron and E. I. Papageorgiou, "Fuzzy grey cognitive maps and nonlinear hebbian learning in process control," *Applied intelligence*, vol. 41, no. 1, pp. 223–234, 2014.

[20] J. W. Forrester, "System dynamics, systems thinking, and soft or," *System dynamics review*, vol. 10, no. 2-3, pp. 245–256, 1994.

[21] G. F. Cooper, "The computational complexity of probabilistic inference using bayesian belief networks," *Artificial intelligence*, vol. 42, no. 2-3, pp. 393–405, 1990.

[22] U. Wilensky and W. Rand, *An introduction to agent-based modeling: modeling natural, social, and engineered complex systems with NetLogo*. Mit Press, 2015.

[23] M. M. Kim and J. Ko, "The impacts of state control policies on college tuition increase," *Educational Policy*, vol. 29, no. 5, pp. 815–838, 2015.

[24] S. W. Hemelt and D. E. Marcotte, "The impact of tuition increases on enrollment at public colleges and universities," *Educational Evaluation and Policy Analysis*, vol. 33, no. 4, pp. 435–457, 2011.

[25] D. E. Heller, "The effects of tuition and state financial aid on public college enrollment," *The Review of Higher Education*, vol. 23, no. 1, pp. 65–89, 1999.

[26] P. T. Brinkman and L. L. Leslie, "Economies of scale in higher education: Sixty years of research," *The review of higher education*, vol. 10, no. 1, pp. 1–28, 1986.

Approach to a Holistic Modelling of Cycling Dynamics

Yannick Rauch
Institute of Energy Efficient Mobility
Karlsruhe University of Applied Science
Karlsruhe, Germany
email: yannick.rauch@h-ka.de

Julia Rall
Mechanical Engineering and Mechatronics
Karlsruhe University of Applied Science
Karlsruhe, Germany
email: julia.rall@outlook.de

Maximilian Ruhe
Mechanical Engineering and Mechatronics
Karlsruhe University of Applied Science
Karlsruhe, Germany
email: maximilian.ruhe@outlook.de

Reiner Kriesten
Institute of Energy Efficient Mobility
Karlsruhe University of Applied Science
Karlsruhe, Germany
email: reiner.kriesten@h-ka.de

***Abstract*—Model-based approaches for the development of complex systems are an established method for component or function development. With an increased interest in cycling due to the political promotion of cycling and the spread of technological innovations, such as e-bikes, model-based approaches can support the corresponding research and development activities, e.g., for a simulation-based assessment of cycling infrastructure. For this purpose, a holistic modelling of bicycle riding should be used, which is able to represent the physical aspects of cycling including a representation of the cyclist, bicycle as well as the environment and dynamics independently. Crucial for such a modelling approach is a comprehensive description of the vehicle's longitudinal, lateral and vertical dynamics as well as its dynamic limitations, which is presented in this paper. Based on a propulsion force given by the overall model, the trajectory and all relevant environmental properties, the resulting model calculates the dynamics relevant for the process of cycling and the cyclist. The necessary parameters are derived from the characteristics of the cyclist and the bicycle as well as the characteristics of the route to be travelled.**

Keywords*—*Cycling; Simulation; Bicycles; Bicycle Dynamics.

I. INTRODUCTION

The consideration and technologisation of cycling and bicycles is an emerging field of interest in research and development applications. On the one hand, an understanding of bicycle usage as well as improvements of the corresponding infrastructure is required to further improve cycling, which is promoted by governments as part of new mobility strategies, e.g., Germany's national cycling plan [1]. On the other hand, new technologies emerge that make the use of bicycles more accessible and convenient, which gets particularly visible in the rapid spread of e-bikes over the last few years [2][3].

To address current research challenges, model-based methods to simulate the whole process of cycling may provide interesting approaches. The utilisation of model-based methods is well established throughout the entire development process of complex systems and software [4], especially in the field of automotive engineering [5]. This makes it possible to test functions or components in the context of an entire vehicle and its environment at early stages of development. For a realistic representation, simulations include a model of the vehicle environment and the driving dynamics according to the physical relationships. Furthermore, there are model-based approaches using a physical-technical description for calculations, e.g., a prediction of electrical energy consumption [6]. However, this extensive use of model-based methods is still fairly uncommon for bicycles.

Possible applications of a physical overall cycling simulation could be the development of functions and components or an energy demand prediction for e-bikes [7][8]. In addition, a holistic modelling of cycling can be used to consider the quality of cycling infrastructure based on variables such as a cyclist's power-/energy expenditure or travel time [9]. In this way, objective aspects of cycling, which can be expressed in physical terms, are made observable from a rider's perspective. For this, a stand-alone simulation must model the rider, the bicycle as well as the environment and the dynamics. The cycling dynamics result from the route and environmental influences as well as the propulsion generated by the cyclist as pedalling torque and bicycle model as propulsion force on the rear wheel, which itself results in relation to the cycling dynamics. Accordingly, this paper presents an approach of a model to simulate the dynamics relevant to the process of cycling and to the cyclist.

Section II provides an overview of the state of the art of cycling model approaches. In Section III, the model of cycling dynamics is derived by physical description and equations. Section IV presents the implementation of the model regarding the resulting model and the required parameters for simulation. Thus, in Section V, the model can be simulated and the corresponding results verified. To conclude, Section VI summarises this paper and provides a preview to future work.

II. State of the Art

The description of the dynamics of cycling primarily needs to consider that a bicycle is a single-track vehicle. Thus, corresponding models exist for the resulting stability problem, as well as associated concepts for the stability control of a bicycle [10], e.g., on the basis of a given steering angle. Furthermore, there are models for describing the resulting vertical dynamics according to the surface profile, for example to represent the comfort of cycling on different road surfaces [11][12]. These modelling approaches can be used, for example, in human-in-the-loop bicycle simulators [13]. This involves generating the feedback of the cycling dynamics according to the human handling and realising it with corresponding actuators. However, modelling approaches that depict a holistic description and representation of a vehicle's longitudinal, lateral and vertical dynamics as well as dynamic limitations are, to the best of our knowledge, not available. Thus, this work proposes an approach for a holistic model of cycling dynamics to be used in a stand-alone model, e.g., to achieve a simulation-based assessment of cycling infrastructure [9]. To realise this, the corresponding physical descriptions found in the literature of bicycle or motorbike technology are used [14][15]. Nevertheless, the corresponding relationships and equations must first be applied to our specific model concept. In addition, the parameters required for the description of the cycling dynamics must be derived from the characteristics of the cyclist and the bicycle.

III. Modelling Cycling Dynamics

To achieve a holistic description for simulating the dynamics of cycling, the model environment provides a simulated propulsion force. The trajectory of the cycled path is given as a-priori knowledge that is derived by the course of the route. Furthermore, the frame of the bicycle is considered inflexible and the cyclists position on the bicycle does not change over the course of a journey. In addition, all further relevant information, e.g., slope, weather/wind, underground, for calculating the dynamics is specified as data given over distance of the route.

Based on these information, the given trajectory and the propulsion force, the resulting model must describe the movement of a cyclist and the bicycle as well as specifying the dynamic limitations of cycling. Accordingly, the necessary description of longitudinal, lateral and vertical dynamics are derived.

A. *Longitudinal Dynamics*

To simulate the process of cycling the description of longitudinal dynamics is a crucial aspect to describe the locomotion of a bicycle and a cyclist. For this the resistance forces of cycling are considered. Thus, the acceleration is calculated on basis of given propulsion $F_{prop.}$ and braking forces F_{brake} on the wheels as well as the resistance forces (1), while the velocity of the bicycle results from the integration of acceleration (2).

$$m\ a = F_{prop.} - F_{brake} - F_{roll} - F_{slope} - F_{drag} \quad (1)$$

$$v(t) = \int a(t)\ dt \quad (2)$$

Accordingly, Figure 1 shows the forces acting on the bicycle and the cyclist as well as the direction of speed and wind.

1) Slope Resistance: For cycling uphill a positive slope value generates the slope resistance force F_{slope}. This refers to the component of gravity F_G depending on the weight of bicycle and cyclist m that occurs in the direction of movement (3). In contrast, this force acts as propulsion when cycling downhill, caused by a negative slope angle α.

$$F_{slope} = F_G\ sin(\alpha)\ = m\ g\ sin(\alpha) \quad (3)$$

2) Drag Resistance: The drag force F_{drag} (4) considers the resistance from the air displacement caused by the movement of bicycle and rider. The front area A depends on the type of the bicycle and the corresponding resulting seating position of cyclists. This also applies to the drag coefficient c_W. In addition, the density of the air ρ_{air} varies according to the altitude, temperature and humidity. Furthermore, the wind can exert a significant force in dependence of the actual wind speed v_{wind}. Thus, the drag force can support or hinder the propulsion depending on the intensity and direction of the wind.

$$F_{drag} = \frac{1}{2}\ \rho_{air}\ c_W\ A\ (v_{bike} - v_{wind})^2 \quad (4)$$

3) Rolling Resistance: Rolling resistance occurs at both wheels of a bicycle and results from flexing, roll off and road resistance. The flexing resistance results from the deformation of the tyres, specifically a flattening around the contact point. The intensity of the deformation and resistance depends on the type of tyre used, in particular its width and profile, as well as the actual tyre pressure. Depending on these properties, the flexing resistance is represented by a factor i_F. Furthermore, the deformation of the tyre causes the contact point of the tyre and the tyre axis to be displaced in relation to each other, so that the normal force F_N generates a torque. This roll off resistance is also represented by a factor c_R, which is calculated according to the distance between the axle and the contact point e (Figure 1) and the wheel radius r_{whl}. The road resistance, which depicts the rolling over the unevenness of a road surface as well as any sinking into the subsoil, is also mapped via a factor i_R. Accordingly, the rolling resistance force F_{roll} (5) is calculated on the basis of the above-mentioned factors as a function of the normal force.

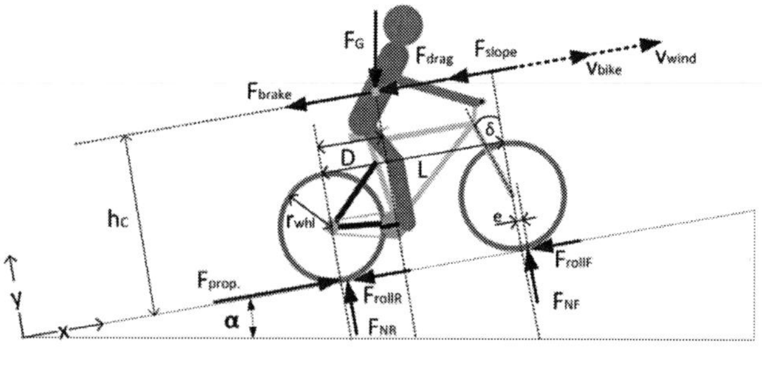

Figure 1. Representation of the dynamics and resistance forces for cycling.

For this purpose, the product of the individual factors can be combined to form the rolling resistance coefficient f_R.

$$F_{roll} = F_N\ i_F\ i_R\ c_R = F_N\ f_R \tag{5}$$

The normal force equals the gravity force in the vertical direction and is thus dependent on the slope angle (6).

$$F_N = F_G\ cos(\alpha)\ = m\ g\ cos(\alpha) \tag{6}$$

4) Transient Resistance: The transient resistance is the force required to overcome the inertia of a vehicle in a direction of motion and of the rotating parts of the power train. Since newtonian mechanics are used to derive the dynamics along the longitudinal axis (1), the mass inertia of the vehicle is already taken into account. In addition, the inertia of the rotating parts of the power train Θ_{PT}, the inertia of front Θ_{FW} and rear wheel Θ_{RW} must be taken into account (7).

$$F_{a,rot} = \frac{\Theta_{PT}\ a}{r_{whl}^2} + \frac{\Theta_{RW}\ a}{r_{whl}^2} + \frac{\Theta_{FW}\ a}{r_{whl}^2} \tag{7}$$

This rotatory acceleration resistance can be added with the translatory resistance ($F_{a,tran} = m\ a_{bike}$) to a total acceleration resistance (8).

$$F_{a,total} = a\ (m + \frac{\Theta_{PT}}{r_{whl}^2} + \frac{\Theta_{RW}}{r_{whl}^2} + \frac{\Theta_{FW}}{r_{whl}^2}) \tag{8}$$

In order to represent the rotational inertia in the given longitudinal dynamic equation (1), a factor λ (9) is used for representation.

$$\lambda = \frac{m + \frac{\Theta_{PT}}{r_{whl}^2} + \frac{\Theta_{RW}}{r_{whl}^2} + \frac{\Theta_{FW}}{r_{whl}^2}}{m} \tag{9}$$

This results in the following equation for the description of the longitudinal dynamics:

$$\lambda\ m\ a = F_{prop.} - F_{brake} - F_{roll} - F_{slope} - F_{drag} \tag{10}$$

B. Lateral Dynamics

Since the proposed cycling model does not deal with the balance or stability control of cycling, the consideration of lateral dynamics emphasis to the resulting movement that occurs in curve situations. In particular, the tilt angle and the steering angle are to be depicted.

1) Bicycle Balance: For the calculation of the tilt angle according to the representation in Figure 2 an ideal curve is assumed. The tilt to a side of the bicycle is caused by a deflection of the centre of gravity in relation to the point of contact. The tilting angle γ of the bicycle is determined by the ratio between the centrifugal force F_C (11) corresponding to the actual curve radius r_c and the normal force F_N.

$$F_C = \frac{m\ v^2}{r_c} \tag{11}$$

These act at a bicycle's centre of gravity and generate a torque around the point of contact corresponding to its height h_c and angular deflection. For stable cornering, these generated torques must be equal (12), so that the tilt angle results (13).

$$F_G\ h_c\ sin(\gamma) = \frac{m\ v^2}{r_c}\ h_c\ cos(\gamma) \tag{12}$$

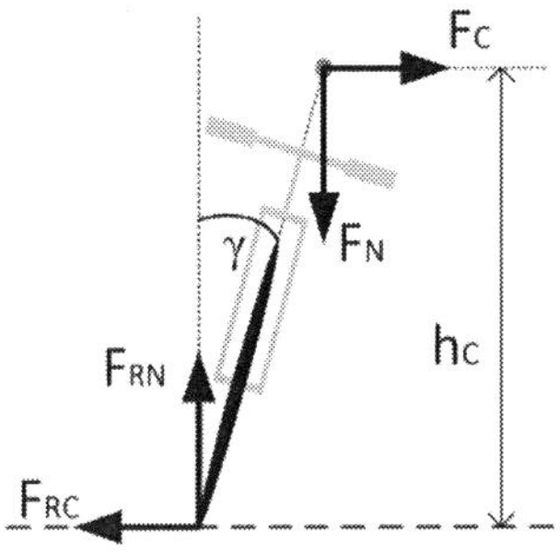

Figure 2. Representation of an idealised stationary cycling trough a curve.

$$tan(\gamma) = \frac{v^2}{g\ r_c} \tag{13}$$

2) Bicycle Steering: In addition to the tilt angle, the handlebars must be turned in for cornering. This steering angle results from the geometry of the vehicle's track model shown in Figure 3. The calculation is based on the yaw angle β (14) around the centre of gravity, the wheelbase L and the distance between the centre of gravity and the rear axle D.

$$sin(\beta) = \frac{D}{r_c} \tag{14}$$

However, this only represents the angle of the front wheel turning from its neutral position ψ (15).

$$tan(\psi) = \frac{L}{D}\ tan(\beta) \tag{15}$$

Based on this, the rotation of the handlebar θ is calculated (16) assuming a small head tube angle δ (Figure 1).

$$tan(\theta) = \frac{\psi}{sin(\delta)} \tag{16}$$

C. Braking Dynamics

For cycling, dynamic limitations occur primarily during the braking process. This is due to the propulsion force that does not usually cause the static friction to be exhausted and thus the wheels to spin. However, when braking intensively, the friction limit is quickly exceeded, so that the corresponding wheel locks up and slips. To enable the cyclist to prevent this, the maximum braking force $F_{B_{max}}$ that can be applied is calculated using the static friction force F_S (17) using the static friction coefficient μ_S as a function of the normal force.

$$F_{B_{max}} = F_S = \mu_S\ F_N = \mu_S\ m\ g\ cos(\alpha) \tag{17}$$

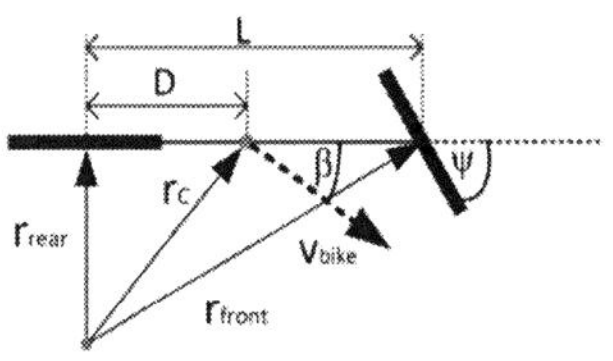

Figure 3. Representation of a bicycle's geometry model for curve cycling.

1) Normal Force Distribution: Furthermore, it must be taken into account that especially during braking there is a nodding movement, which is caused by the mass inertia/acceleration. This leads to an increase in the front wheel load and a reduction in the rear wheel load. The wheel loads at the front/rear wheel (19)/(18) can be calculated from the moment equilibria corresponding to the normal forces (6) and the inertia force resulting from the acceleration.

$$F_{N_{front}} = \frac{F_N \; D - m \; a \; h_S}{L} \tag{18}$$

$$F_{N_{rear}} = \frac{F_N \; (L - D) + m \; a \; h_S}{L} \tag{19}$$

Applied to (17), this results in different maximum braking forces for the front and rear wheel.

2) Braking in Curve Situations: Braking during cornering is subjected to further limitations, so that the maximum possible braking force is decreased accordingly. This is due to the existing static friction force being used for lateral traction (20). As lateral guidance force, the centrifugal force must be applied.

$$F_{B_{max}} = \sqrt{F_S^2 - F_C^2} \tag{20}$$

To calculate the maximum braking force on the front/rear wheel, the centrifugal forces must be calculated based on the weight distribution, the speed and the corresponding curve radius. The curve radius of the front and rear wheel result from the geometry of the bicycle (Figure 3). The equivalent masses for front and rear wheel result according to the position of the centre of gravity on the longitudinal axis. With the resulting centrifugal/lateral guidance forces (21)/(22), the maximum braking force for front/rear wheel can be calculated (20).

$$F_{C_{front}} = \frac{m \; D \; v^2}{L \; \sqrt{r_c^2 - D^2 + L^2}} \tag{21}$$

$$F_{C_{rear}} = \frac{m \; (L - D) \; v^2}{L \; \sqrt{r_c^2 - D^2}} \tag{22}$$

D. Vertical Dynamics

The vertical dynamics represent the effects of the road surface on the cyclist. For this purpose, the tyre and the suspension fork are modelled as a serially connected spring-damper unit for the front axle, while only the tyre is modelled for the rear axle. According to a given profile of the underground, the deflection passed on to the respective wheel can thus be calculated.

IV. Implementation

The physical equations given from literature and the description of the dynamics of cycling derived from those are modelled in *MATLAB/Simulink* and simulated with the numerical methods offered there. This results in our definition of an overall structure of the dynamics model. In addition, the parameters used for the modelling must be provided and determined.

A. Resulting Model

The resulting model is presented in Figure 4 and consists of five subsystems. According to the formulated description of the driving dynamics, all quantities are handled as scalars and apply in the direction defined in the corresponding figures (Figure 1, 2, 3). The longitudinal dynamics system calculates the acceleration and velocity of the bicycle according to the slope angle α_{slope}, the roll resistance factor f_R, the resulting wind speed v_{wind}, the density of the air ρ_{air} and a given propulsion force $F_{propulsion}$. The gravity subsystem calculates the normal forces for front and rear wheel $F_{N_{front}}/F_{N_{rear}}$ by considering the slope angle and the acceleration of the bicycle. The curve dynamics use the bicycles velocity and the curve radius r_{curve} (measured to the centre of gravity) and include the calculation of steering angles ϕ, θ, the tilt angle γ as well as the centrifugal forces at front and rear wheel $F_{C_{front}}/F_{C_{rear}}$. In combination with the normal forces these are considered by the braking subsystem to calculate the maximum braking forces for each wheel $F_{B_{max,front}}/F_{B_{max,rear}}$. The vertical dynamics use the calculated normal forces to determine the translation/deflection passed on to the front and rear wheel y_{front}/y_{rear} which can be given by a road surface profile.

B. Modelling Parameters

The required parameters are calculated from the characteristics of the rider, bicycle and the route. A distinction is made between parameters that are variable over the course of the route and those that are constant for a ride. Both the constant parameters and the parameters depicted over the route are calculated by appropriate pre-processing before the simulation is executed. In order to retrieve the distance-dependent parameters, the distance travelled so far on the given route is required. For this purpose, the model of the longitudinal dynamics is extended by the integration of the velocity over the simulation time.

1) Ride Constant Parameter: To calculate the ride constant parameters, it is assumed that the characteristics of the rider and bicycle are sufficiently known. Among other things, the total weight of rider and bicycle must be calculated. The parameters for the aerodynamic description, c_W-value and frontal area A, are determined depending on the type of bicycle used, e.g., mountain bike (MTB) or road bike and the physique of the rider. In the same way, the centre of gravity

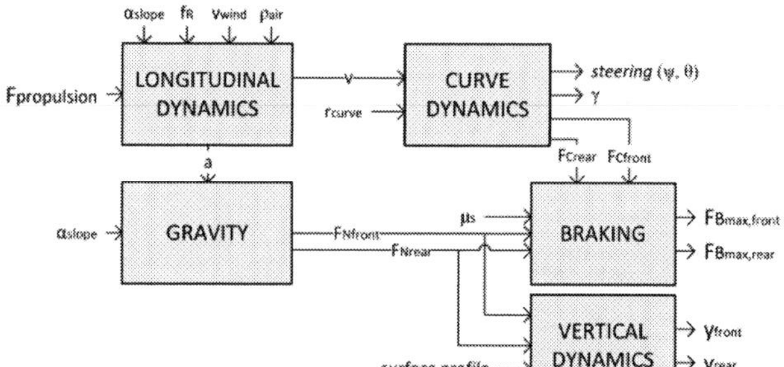

Figure 4. Resulting approach of a holistic dynamic model of cycling.

position h_S, D can be derived, while the head tube angle δ and wheelbase L are only determined on the basis of the bicycle used. The parameters describing the spring-damper unit should also be derived according to the bicycle type, while the vertical dynamic properties of the tyres are calculated depending on the type, e.g., MTB or road bike tyres, as well as the tyre pressure. For a general consideration, the derivation of the parameter values is based on defined rules, whereas for a concrete bicycle these data can be specified individually.

2) Distance Dependent Parameter: For synthetic routes, the user must define the required properties, whereas for routes based on real infrastructure, tools and methods for route data generation can be used. In our case, a self-developed route data generation algorithm and environment is used that has been applied to the application for bicycles [16].

This tool enables the calculation of the curve radius r_{curve} and the altitude profile of the route, from which the slope angle α_{slope} can be calculated. The air pressure ρ_{air} is calculated depending on the altitude profile and the generated air pressure, humidity and temperature. The resulting wind speed v_{wind} is calculated according to the general wind speed and direction as well as the trajectory. The rolling resistance f_R and the static friction coefficient μ_S depend on the surface, but also on the type of tyre and its pressure.

C. Determination of Parameters

For the modelling of the cycling dynamics of a bicycle it should be possible to depict specific bicycles as well as generic bicycle types.

1) Parameters for Specific Bicycles: The geometric data as well as the weight can be taken from the technical data for a known bicycle or measured directly. The required characteristics for modelling the specific spring-damper unit, are usually not publicly available. However, the specific values are only required if the vertical dynamics are to be considered in detail.

Furthermore, experiments can be realised to determine parameters of longitudinal dynamics, for example a coasting test to determine the drag coefficients ($c_W A$) and the rolling resistance coefficient (f_R). For this purpose, the coasting process on a flat road, in which only the air and rolling resistance act, is simulated using (1) and (2) with a given initial speed. The searched parameters are iterated and the mean square error between simulated and measured speed is calculated. Based on the parameter combination with the smallest error, the drag and the rolling resistance coefficient for the given surface are obtained, as shown in Figure 5.

2) Parameters for Generic Bicycles: The required database for deriving the dynamic parameters on the basis of the bicycle or tyre type is derived from literature and the results of experiments. Assumptions are also made according to qualitative data from literature, which in turn must be evaluated through experimental tests. To determine the geometric information, data sheets can be used from which average values can be obtained. For the description of the spring-damper unit, standard values are used, which result from components specific to the type of vehicle.

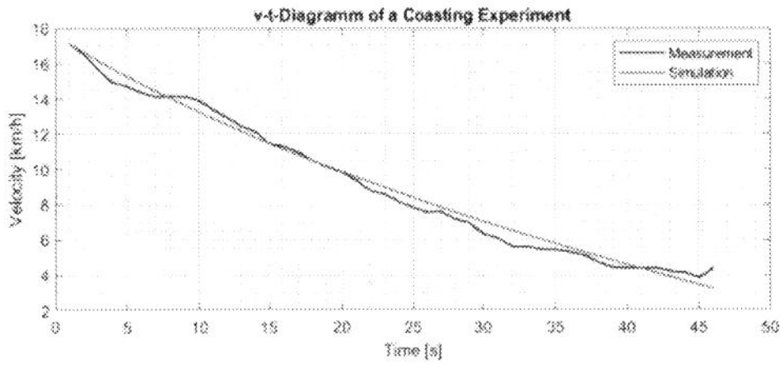

Figure 5. Coasting experiment to determine parameters of longitudinal dynamics (f_R= 0.006, $c_W A$ = 0.6 m²).

V. SIMULATION AND RESULTS

To verify whether the developed dynamics model is correctly formulated, it is integrated into the model environment in *Simulink*. This simulates the propulsion force applied to the rear wheel and provides the required route data, such as the parameters for calculating the longitudinal dynamics. Figure 6 shows the corresponding results for driving on a forest road. The first part of the route is uphill, which is reflected in the gradient resistance and plausibly results in a lower speed. As soon as the uphill and overall resistance decreases, the speed increases as expected. Furthermore, it shows correctly that the increased velocity neutralises the tailwind that acts on the cyclist in the course of the ride. To demonstrate the dynamics of cycling curves Figure 7 illustrates this process. Therefore a curve radius between 10 to 30 meters is given and the resulting tilt and steering angles are displayed. It can therefore be shown that, as expected, narrower curves or smaller curve radii result in increased steering and tilt angles.

Figure 8 shows forces involved in the breaking process on front and rear wheel. For this purpose, the brakes are applied from a speed of 24 km/h while driving through a curve with a radius of 100 metres and, for illustration purposes, a high static friction value of 0.98 is selected. It can be seen that plausibly an increased load is applied to the front wheel due to the deceleration and thus an increased maximum braking force occurs.

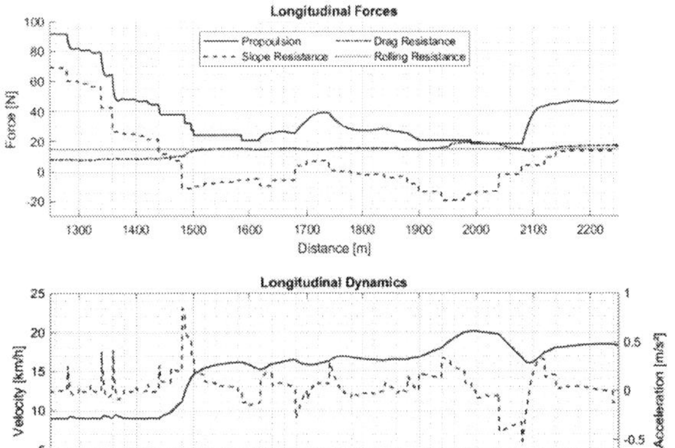

Figure 6. Results of the subsystem for calculating the longitudinal dynamics of cycling on a forest road.

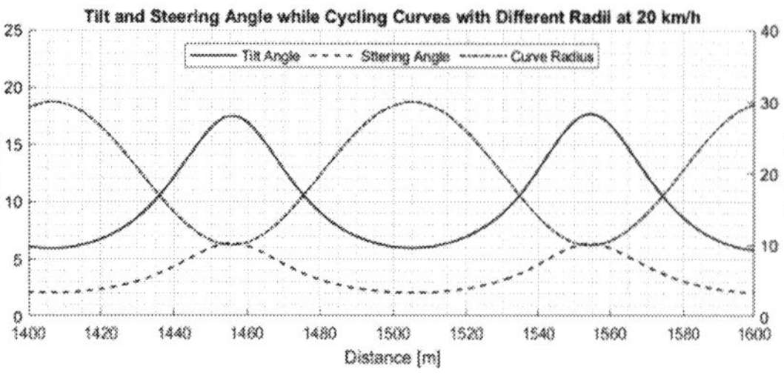

Figure 7. Results of the subsystem for calculating the dynamics of curve cycling.

As expected, an opposite effect appears at the rear wheel. Furthermore, the model correctly represents that the decreasing centrifugal force caused by the reduced speed on both wheels leads to an increase of the maximum braking force.

VI. Conclusion and Future Work

This paper presents an approach towards a holistic model of cycling dynamics to be used for simulating the whole process of cycling, e.g., to be used for the assessment of cycling infrastructure. Therefore the proposed model calculates the longitudinal, lateral and vertical dynamics as well as dynamic limitations as a function of a given propulsion force and trajectory. Furthermore, all relevant parameter describing the route, the cyclist or the bicycle are available as a-priori knowledge. Accordingly, physical descriptions of the cycling process provided by literature are applied to achieve a suitable model for given use-cases, e.g., a model-based assessment of cycling infrastructure. Additionally a brief overview of the determination of these parameters for specific and generic bicycles is provided. The resulting model is implemented as a *Simulink* model while the required parameters are calculated by pre-processing functions. Thus, a verification shows that the developed model is capable of plausibly representing the required representation of cycling dynamics.

Further development of the model will mainly focus on the qualitative evaluation of the model. Literature research and experiments will be used to develop functions for determining

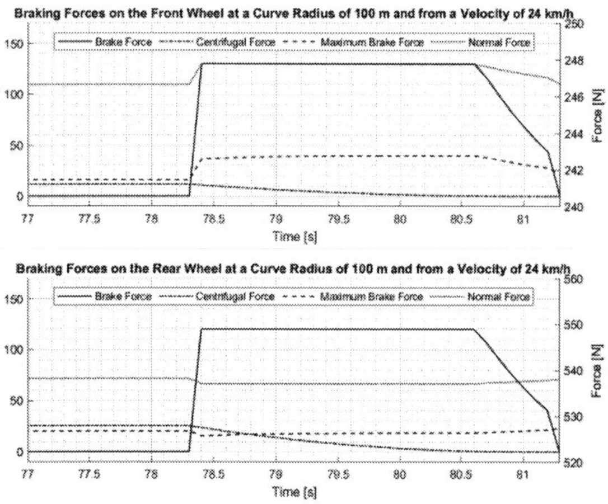

Figure 8. Results of the forces involved in braking dynamics.

the required parameters. Once the parameters have been determined precisely, an extended evaluation of the dynamics model can be carried out especially in comparison to real cycling situations. Furthermore, optimisations of individual subsystems are possible as well as a continuous development of the model according to given requirements from the model environment or given use-cases.

Acknowledgment

This work was carried out as part of MODELO-Rad project [9], sponsored by the Ministry of Digitalisation and Traffic of the Federal Republic of Germany.

References

[1] Federal Ministry for Digital and Transport, "National Cycling Plan 3.0," 2021.

[2] Zweirad-Industrie-Verband e.V., "Market data bicycles and e-bikes 2022 - Marktdaten Fahrräder und E-Bikes 2022," 2023.

[3] Royal RAI Association, "Mobility in Figures Two-Wheelers," 2023, [Online]. Available from: https://www.raivereniging.nl/file/upload/doc/clickable-pdf-mic-mobiliteit-in-cijfers-tweewielers-2022-1.pdf 2023.08.04.

[4] M. Glöckler, "Simulation als Teil moderner Entwicklungsprozesse," in *Simulation mechatronischer Systeme*, ser. Lehrbuch, M. Glöckler, Ed. Springer Vieweg, 2018, pp. 251–261.

[5] J. Schäuffele and T. Zurawka, *Automotive Software Engineering*. Wiesbaden: Springer Fachmedien Wiesbaden, 2013.

[6] K. Kruppok, C. Gutenkunst, R. Kriesten, and E. Sax, "Prediction of energy consumption for an automatic ancillary unit regulation," in *17. Internationales Stuttgarter Symposium*, ser. Proceedings, M. Bargende, H.-C. Reuss, and J. Wiedemann, Eds. Springer Fachmedien Wiesbaden, 2017, pp. 41–56.

[7] E. Burani, G. Cabri, and M. Leoncini, "An Algorithm to Predict E-Bike Power Consumption Based on Planned Routes," *Electronics*, vol. 11, no. 7, p. 1105, 2022.

[8] Y. Rauch and F. May, "Online Energy and Range Prediction for E-Bikes," in *Reports on Energy Efficient Mobility – Volume 3*, D. Feßler, M. Kettner, R. Kriesten, P. Nenninger, and P. Offermann, Eds. Zenodo, 2023, pp. 100–110.

[9] J. Eckart, R. Kriesten, and Y. Rauch. (2022) Modelo-Rad. [Online]. Available from: https://www.mobilitaetsforum.bund.de/DE/Themen/Wissenspool/Projekte/Projektbeispiele/Projekte/MODELO_Rad.html 2023.08.04.

[10] A. L. Schwab and J. P. Meijaard, "A review on bicycle dynamics and rider control," *Vehicle System Dynamics*, vol. 51, no. 7, pp. 1059–1090, 2013.

[11] W. Du, D. Zhang, and X. Zhao, "Dynamic modelling and simulation of electric bicycle ride comfort," in *2009 International Conference on Mechatronics and Automation*. IEEE, 2009, pp. 4339–4343.

[12] C.-P. Chou *et al.*, "Simulation of Bicycle-Riding Smoothness by Bicycle Motion Analysis Model," *Journal of Transportation Engineering*, vol. 141, no. 12, p. 04015031, 2015.

[13] D.-S. Kwon *et al.*, "KAIST interactive bicycle racing simulator: the 2nd version with advanced features," in *IEEE/RSJ International Conference on Intelligent Robots and System*. IEEE, 2002, pp. 2961–2966.

[14] M. Gressmann, *Bicycle Physics and Biomechanics - Fahrradphysik und Biomechanik: Technik - Formeln - Gesetze*, 12th ed., ser. Tour. Bielefeld: Delius Klasing Verlag, 2017.

[15] J. Stoffregen, *Motorradtechnik*. Wiesbaden: Vieweg+Teubner Verlag, 2012.

[16] T. Nguyen and Y. Rauch, "Real Route Generation for Simulation Based Developement," in *Reports on Energy Efficient Mobility – Volume 2*, D. Feßler, M. Kettner, R. Kriesten, P. Nenninger, and P. Offermann, Eds. Zenodo, 2022, pp. 58–64.

Real World Case Study To Teach Simulation

Lara Zakfeld, Carlo Simon, Merlin Hladik and Stefan Haag

Hochschule Worms
Erenburgerstr. 19, 67549 Worms, Germany
Email: {zakfeld, simon, merlin.hladik, haag}@hs-worms.de

***Abstract*—Classical lectures, supplementary reading and best practice demonstrations (often) form the core of traditional teaching. This is appropriate for the education of syntax and semantics of a process modelling language and to conduct simulation. They are, however, inappropriate to convey pragmatics. But exactly this is needed to stimulate discrete thinking and creativity, skills required in business for the challenges of digitalization in a professional environment. This paper is about using a real world case study to teach modelling and simulation of processes and to facilitate students with the ability to find solutions on their own. Students are confronted with the challenges as they actually occur. They have to face the needs of stakeholders which means that in addition to the actual simulation model, also an interface must be developed for the input of the simulation parameters and a dashboard for the presentation of the simulation results. The danger of this approach is to overburden students with the multitude of tasks required for a solution, potentially leading to a failure of the teaching process. At a glance, the paper summarizes the teaching material developed and the experiences made so far with this approach.**

***Keywords*—Interactive Education; Real World Case Study; Modeling; Petri Nets; Simulation.**

I. Introduction

The learning pyramid as depicted in Figure 1 classifies different teaching approaches and the corresponding learners' retention rates. The most active and participative methods show the highest learning coefficients [1]. The more teaching concepts shift to problem solving, the higher the average retention rate of the method is.

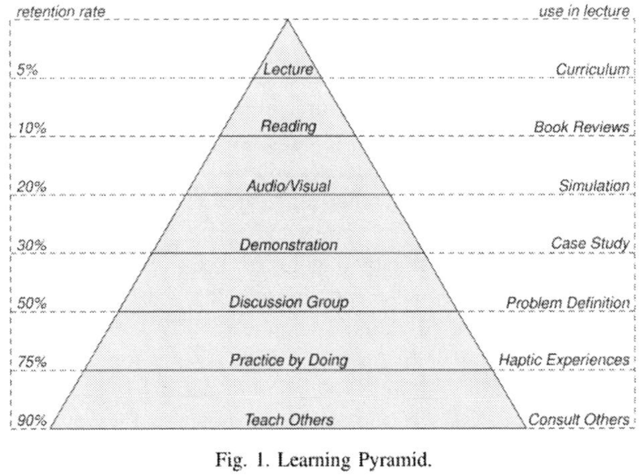

Fig. 1. Learning Pyramid.

Each layer of the pyramid follows a different didactic approach and indicates which retention rate can be expected from the students [2]. This paper is about a method to increase the retention rate of case studies by using a real world example of a consulting project the authors have conducted. The aim of this approach is to convey the complex reality into teaching. With this way of teaching, the authors want to motivate the students to answer the question of why they should learn a specific topic: the answer is to be able to satisfy the customers' needs later on in a business context.

The wish to offer such kinds of lectures results from the very specific idea of Universities of Applied Sciences (UAS) in Germany (like Hochschule Worms). They differ from „Classic" Universities (CU) as they are also known in other countries.

In addition to scientific reputation, UAS lecturers must have practical work experience and circulate this hands-on knowledge to their students to prepare them for an industry career. Further, they are encouraged to maintain industry contacts to exchange ideas, keep their own research and teaching up to date, and conduct practical industry research projects. At the other end, CU professors would rather conduct fundamental research, which is also reflected in their teaching. Boundaries between the two types of universities are fluid [3].

UAS tend to a learning environment with small class sizes, are often more hands-on, and include practical projects and group work. The Hochschule Worms, for example, claims these ideas in its strategy: research and practice guide the teaching to increase competence in students' careers and academics [4]. The aim of this approach is to expand the students' knowledge and enable them to solve problems on the basis of the newly acquired knowledge [5].

Several teaching concepts have been presented at the SIMUL 2022 conference ([2][6]), sparking an intensive discussion about what lecturers do to improve their lecturing: What further interactive methods for teaching modeling and simulation are needed? This contribution continues the discussion started one year ago.

New ideas to develop teaching further is discussed at the example of process management as an important pillar in business informatics studies. Process models help to understand, optimize and automate processes in detail. Thus, they are an essential foundation of the fourth industrial revolution for the digital transformation of companies. However, books and other classic teaching media are only partially successful in conveying the special features of processes within dynamic systems. Simulation based teaching combined with a real world case study has the potential to lift the teaching success to a higher level.

A real world case study on process modeling and simulation which also includes requirements of practitioners offers the chance to develop the following competencies [7]:

1) Systems Competence
2) Decision-making Competence
3) Future & Design Competence

The following Section II outlines the real world case study. Then, Section III explains the shift from the real world to a digital world. Afterwards, Section IV shows how to model processes and design an interface to control the simulation. The actual simulation is discussed in Section V. The translation of the mathematical results into a dashboard is explained in Section VI. A conclusion ends the paper.

II. Real World Case Study

Modeling and simulation play a crucial role in business and especially in logistics, but need skilled people who are able to develop and run the models. Future-oriented skills must be taught for this [7]: *System Competence* is an indispensable precondition to conduct process simulation. It trains students to understand systems and their interdependence. Part of this knowledge is how to design, implement and monitor processes. This competence goes hand in hand with the *Decision-making Competence*. It involves considering different alternatives against each other. As soon as students model and simulate processes, they develop the competence to decide and act responsible. Finally, simulation trains the willingness to change and to think ahead as envisaged in the *Future & Design Competence*. Based on simulation, students can further develop scenarios and creatively solve problems. Considering the learning pyramid of [1], it is important to embed these skills into an experience-based learning environment, such as case studies.

In principle, companies use case studies to explain their products in order to market them afterwards. Those studies show the impact of commerce on the end result and tell how real customers overcame their problems with the product or service offered. In the context of teaching, lecturers successfully apply such aspects as storytelling, overcoming problems, or cause-and-effect principles in teaching. Real world case studies allow students to recreate challenges they will face in their future work [8]. The gap between theory and practice is closed [9].

Real world case studies are discussed in literature several times like in [8], [10], [11] or [12]. They are characterized by the fact that concrete problems are conveyed to students for analysis, open discussion, and final debate. It requires five steps to design a case study [13]:

1) The focus of the analysis is the actual situation.
2) The academic focus of knowledge must be put into action.
3) Students are intellectually and emotionally involved in the method.
4) Lecturers act as facilitators and must be both teacher and practitioner.
5) Students develop an interdisciplinary understanding of the problem.

The actual situation in this case study chosen by the authors is as follows: Infraserv Logistics (ISL) at Industriepark Höchst expands its logistics services for the chemical, pharmaceutical and healthcare industries [14]. A new warehouse is built and the operation starts. Safety requirements have top priority.

With the new warehouse, ISL sets new standards in the efficient, largely digitized storage of highly dangerous goods. To meet these standards across the industry, the industrial park provides information concerning the pilot phase of the warehouse to this real world case study. Only concrete specifications of transport times within the warehouse are dissembled with respect to the competitive situation.

The goal of the conducted modeling and simulation is to objectify assumptions made during the conceptual phase. ISL wants to use simulation to find its own best practices and seeks verification from external parties. The core task of the case study is to model and simulate the core processes in the warehouse. Among other things, the following data is provided for this purpose:

- Space for more than 25,000 pallets
- 9 separate warehouse sections
- Storage of multiple LGK storage classes
- A wide temperature range from -6 to 20 degrees Celsius in the different sections of the warehouse [14]

Some of the data is publicly available in press reports or on the website. All other sensitive data needed to successfully model and simulate the processes are known to the authors but had to be modified for this publication for the above mentioned reasons to guarantee the trust of the industry partner.

III. From Real To Digital World

The first step in modelling a real world warehouse is to collect the relevant real data and to build a digital shadow of the warehouse which can be simulated [15]. The digital shadow serves as the overarching concept. It does not only map real processes into a virtual world but can also use the real world data as input for the simulation.

The first choice to be made is that of an appropriate modelling language and simulation environment. In this course the choice is done by the lecturer in order to synchronize the individual learning processes of the students' groups.

Petri nets have been chosen due to their mathematical basis. They differ from other languages in their possibilities for analysis, simulation and immediate feasibility in a target system. A suitable tool for this is the *Process-Simulations.Center (P-S.C)*. In addition to its already presented features [6], the tool's connectability to external data has been expanded. By entering data in a customer-specific input mask, it is possible to directly access a place in the Petri net model of the warehouse, as shown in Figure 2.

As already mentioned, the case study contains sensitive real world data. Therefore, access and visibility must be limited,

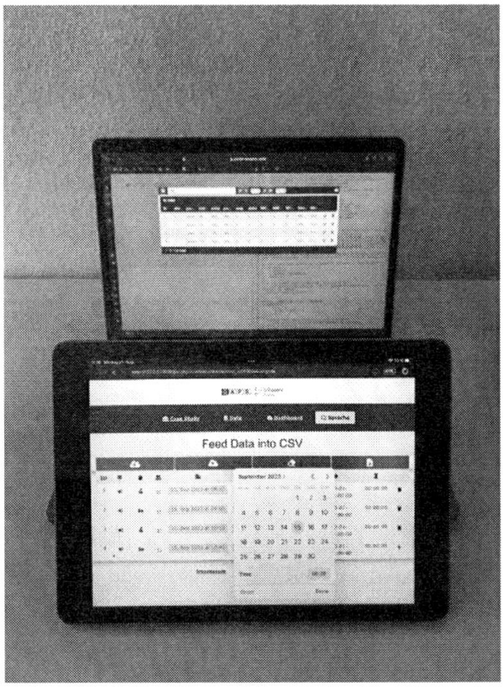

Fig. 2. Interface between Real World and Digital World.

especially for sensitive customer data. Here, the *P-S.C-Cloud* as well as the multi-client capability of the tool helps to manage security issues [6]. Sensitive input data and simulation results can be stored on in-house servers independent from the *P-S.C-Cloud* as explained next.

The close collaboration of real and digital world is shown in Figure 3. The dashed line shows the interface between the local UI of the end-users (of the partner company or the students) and the *P-S.C-Cloud*. This interface allows to drive the simulation with real world data in consulting projects and with modified data during lectures. The latter is defined in a way that still gives the students a comprehension of the entire system. In consequence, as the modelled system becomes more complex, the skill requirements of the students increase.

The phases of the interaction between the local UI and the *P-S.C* can be explained as follows:

Feed: The process starts with the end users of the simulation, i.e., engineers or during operation the warehouse manager or students who play this role in the lecture. They use a customized input mask to enter order data and available resources for a simulation run. All they need for this is a browser on a computer or even an iPad like the warehouse employees use on the shop floor. This data is stored in a CSV file on a company's local server. The *P-S.C* uses a link to load the data into the simulation.

Run simulation: The simulation is conducted on the base of the linked input data. If necessary, the link to the input data can be hid from unauthorized users. The input data is loaded

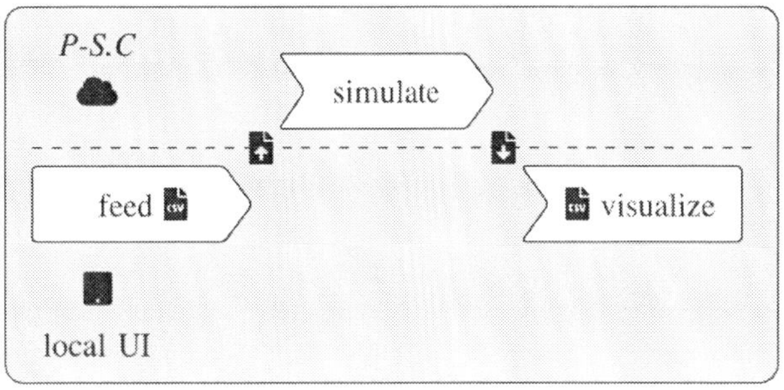

Fig. 3. Real World vs. Digital World.

directly into the browser of the end user, i.e., the *P-S.C-Cloud* does not get in touch with this data. After the simulation has finished, an automatic download is started and the users can store the simulation result on their local computer.

Visualize: The downloaded CSV file in turn can now be uploaded again in the local UI or another business intelligence application. The simulation results are visualized in a way that supports the end users to come to a decision on how to proceed in the real world.

In guided student projects, all of the following aspects can be discussed and worked on, which are formulated as todos:

1) Identify the process to transfer pallets into and out of the stock.
2) Specify the data necessary to control this process.
3) Develop a data driven model for the process.
4) Develop a user interface to administrate the simulation input data.
5) Develop a user interface to visualize the simulation results.

Different abilities and skills are demanded for this complex list of tasks: the students should have previous knowledge and practical experience in programming. They should be able to develop user interfaces and visualize data in diagrams. Hence, the described tasks are part of an advanced concept. In the context of lectures, a high level of training of the students as well as assistance for a satisfying solution is required. Once the infrastructure depicted in Figure 3 has been developed, different scenarios can be simulated and suggestions to improve the real world process can be systematically be derived from the simulation run.

IV. Feed - Processes and Data

According to the list of activities named in the previous section, the work on the following three activities merges together into one large task:

- Identify the process to transfer pallets into and out of the stock.
- Specify the data necessary to control this process.
- Develop a user interface to administrate the simulation input data.

The goal is to have an end user friendly interface to administrate the simulation relevant data. This data will control the simulation run. The virtual order will then run through the simulation model and its processing proceeds. This progress needs to be documented such that there must be a data field within the order that codifies the current state. The naming of these states is deferred to the next section.

The second aspect is that there are two major movements within a warehouse: goods are transferred to stock, inbound, and are released from stock, outbound. Hence, also an attribute is needed to codify the direction of movement. Finally, since the simulation result has to be visualized in a dashboard, an attribute must be reserved to document the duration of each task.

Further attributes are those that control the process flow like the arrival time of trucks, the loading ramp to choose, or the staging time for material. To find these attributes, students read through the case study and conduct on-site (or virtual) interviews. A challenging task is to determine a good degree of detail. For the learning success on understanding the complexity of systems, it is crucial to maintain authenticity.

Subsequently, the focus lies on the interface. It is important to stay close to the customer's needs. The interface of the application is initially programmed bilingual in English and German. The input mask shown on an iPad in Figure 2 and as a screenshot in Figure 4 are examples on how the user interface may look like. Here, nudging and the poke-yoke effect are of great assistance. Both ensure that only target-oriented and required data are entered by the users.

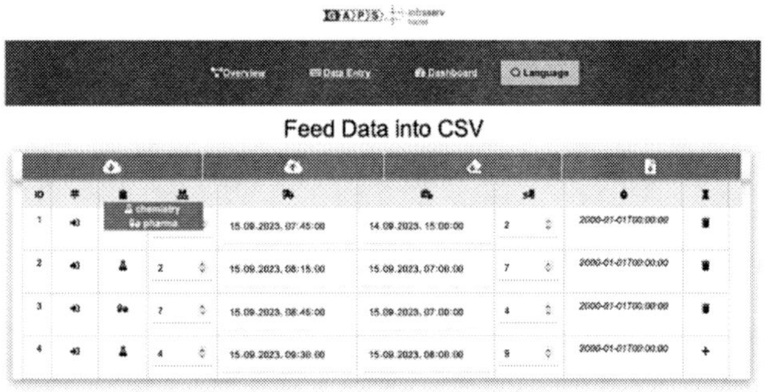

Fig. 4. Feed Data into CSV.

The input mask has a variety of functions:

- Load the last uploaded data
- Upload data (e.g., to the *P-S.C-Cloud*)
- Remove data
- Download data locally
- + Add a data set

The CSV file to control the *P-S.C*-simulation can be generated with this user interface. For this, a place representing the orders of the warehouse are typed in a similar way. At the beginning of the simulation, the data can be loaded from a (company's) web server using a link to the file.

V. SIMULATE - SIMULATION TO CSV

The results of the last phase, interface and data structure, are now used to develop the simulation model. This work package includes several student activities from Section III. The data structure plays a crucial role, as it links the phases. The starting point here are also the real processes to inbound and outbound pallets in the warehouse. First, the process steps need to be identified in order to reduce the complexity of the overall processes to single states. The different states are shown in Table I and Table II.

TABLE I. STATES WITHIN THE ORDER PLACE DURING INBOUND

State	Description
scheduled	Order booked into LAP
arrived	Truck arrived at warehouse
registering	Truck is registering
docking	Truck at ramp
unloading	Truck unloades pallet by pallet
undocking	Truck leaves ramp
leaving	Truck left ramp
departed	Truck left yard & Order released
storaging	Goods are being stored
finished	Goods are in storage

TABLE II. STATES WITHIN THE ORDER PLACE DURING OUTBOUND

State	Description
scheduled	Order booked into LAP
staging	Goods are taken from storage
completed	Staging is completed
arrived	Truck arrived at warehouse
registering	Truck registered on the yard
docking	Truck arrived at warehouse
loading	Truck is loaded pallet by pallet
undocking	Truck leaves ramp
leaving	Truck left ramp
departed	Truck left yard

Besides the state changes of the orders the execution of the orders is controlled by the available resources, such as type and kind of forklifts. In ISL's new warehouse, there are two types of forklifts - *SGS* for high-bay movements and *VHS*, which move on the shopfloor. These forklifts add more states and transitions to the Petri net. Forklifts remove the goods from the truck, transfer them from the ramp to the staging area, and finally via the transfer area into the high rack.

Such state transitions involving multiple resources are displayed in Figures 5 and 6. Both figures are parallel finite-state machines with prioritized resources. The previous tables, but also the finite-state machine, help during modeling to become aware of the individual states of the orders, forklifts and other resources.

All forklifts, especially VHS, are in a competitive situation with each other. The allocation takes place as seen in the finite state machine at state *i5* for inbound (Figure 5) and state *o8* for outbound (Figure 6). Further, the transition *next*, shown in Figure 7 organizes and sorts the orders according to the requirements of the warehouse managers. The data of the orders as well as the resources control the processes in the simulation.

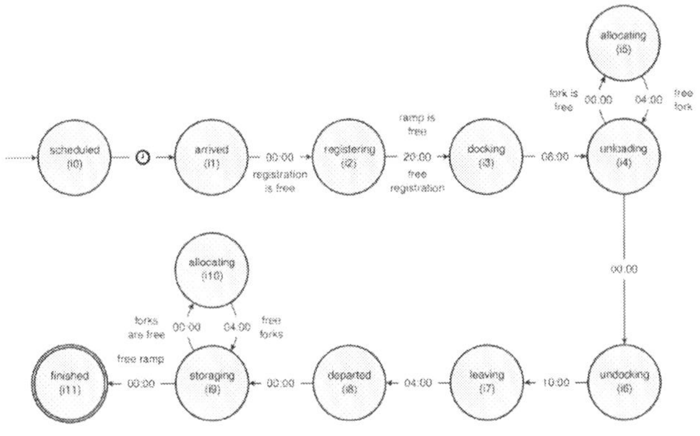

Fig. 5. Finite-state machine - Inbound.

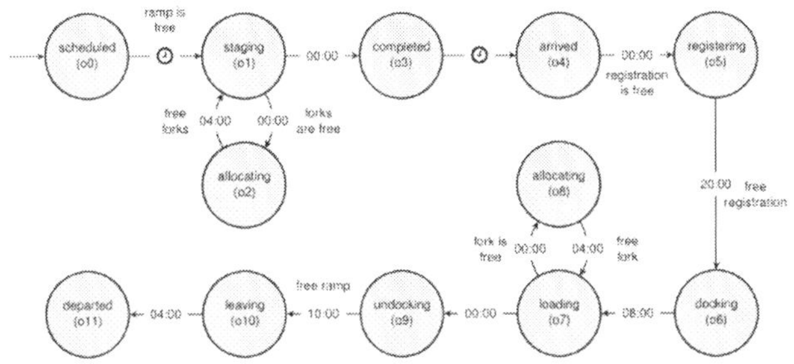

Fig. 6. Finite-state machine - Outbound.

A central clock synchronizes the activities as already described in [16]. This clock increases only, if all activities for a specific moment in time have been finished. The time at which an specific state transition is conducted is documented within a timestamp.

Figure 7 shows the setup of the Petri net and the clock mechanism at the same time. While the simulation runs, the orders change. Each change is copied into a protocol file, also in CSV-format. And this file is the input for the next step.

VI. Visualize - CSV To Visualization

This final step completes the students' work. This step involves the development of a user interface to visualize the simulation results. Firstly, students draw insights from working with the project partner, as well as its real world challenges. Secondly, part of the education includes research in professional literature. Third, students learn with each model or dashboard they create. For example, the students are sensitized to choose the right format (16:9 or 9:16) or provide the most accessible frame, such as a CSV file to enter, process or visualize data. Practice literature like [17] clearly elaborates on the benefits and features of useful dashboards: dashboards serve to create a coherent and coordinated picture that allows users to see and understand data.

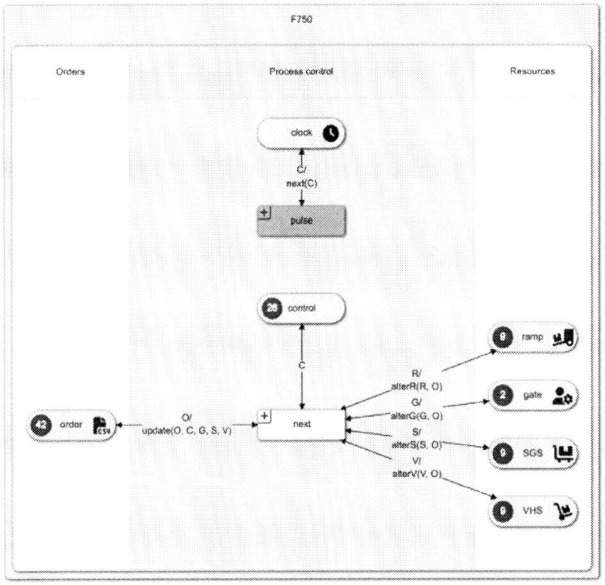

Fig. 7. Screenshot Petri net model by *P-S.C.*

On this basis, the dashboard of Figure 8 offers a step towards more objectivity and thus addresses the needs of the project partner. In addition, the dashboard now unites all parts of the warehouse - from registration to the high-bay warehouse. Therefore, this dashboard is the evolution of the last dashboard shown in [6].

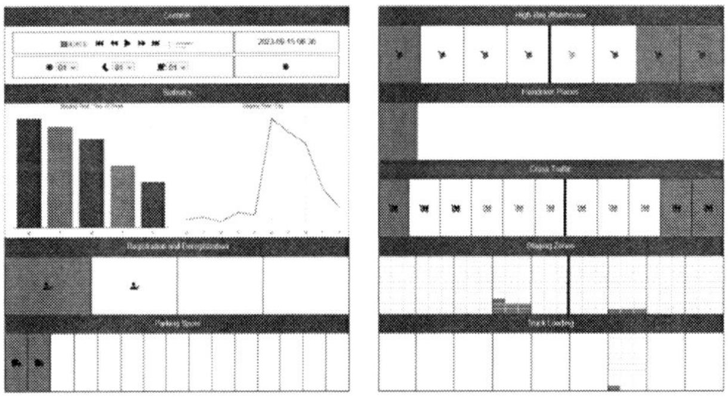

Fig. 8. Interactive Dashboard.

The strategy behind this dashboard is that all information is visible in one place. It combines recognition and objectivity: users have to recognize their processes and the orders flowing along these processes. Symbols within the dashboard help to keep track of the things. With a rising complexity, these additional symbols might deviate from what is important.

Further Few (2013) reminds to design dashboards, such that users are able to understand and interpret the data - this is more than just to see it [17]. Based on this, the authors recommend that students do not visualize the movement of forklifts and trucks as described in [6] or as is popular with 3D animation software. Such animations also became less important for the project partner as the project progressed and the dashboard could be observed along with the real world as its shadow.

The board can be divided into several parts:

- An interactive control panel is located at the top left. Users may control the speed of the visualization, or pause it at interesting moments. Further aspects like opening hours for externals, closing times, preparatory times can be controlled here.
- Below of the control panel, an analytic's board shows varies statics concerning the processes like staging time over the period of a work week. This information can be presented in different types of charts.
- The remaining areas of the dashboard belong to the different areas of the warehouse, from registration to high rack. Chemical and pharmaceutical goods are separated. Within each area, the amount of disposable is shown. When the visualization is started, the staffing of resources and their allocation by orders is presented over time.

The remaining area presents the following information:

- Ramps quantity and allocation
- Forklift quantity including buffer space
- Parking slots for waiting trucks
- Truck load limit
- Number of employees for registration

This setting is ideal for both, the employees in the company and the students, to "play" with the data and to observe how the performance of the warehouse changes with changing capacities of the various resources. Resources that are underutilized or bottlenecks can be identified.

VII. Conclusion and Outlook

Taking a real world scenario and putting it into a classroom is a challenging task. Details hinder the students from having easy and simple solutions. But this experience is very important for young people being prepared for the challenges of a digitalized world.

The case study helps to develop critical competencies:

- Understand the benefit of modeling and simulation.
- Build models of the real world that can be simulated as their shadows.
- Understand the purpose of a valuable dashboard.
- Learn how to design a dashboard.
- Link a dashboard with the simulation results.
- And learn how to explain each single step.

The authors had to recognize that only the best Bachelor students were able to follow the entire story. And even using transformer AI-technologies do not help to ease this task at the moment [18]. For this reason they do not plan to complicate the scenario and simulation further more.

The next objective is to publish the use case in the tutorial to the *P-S.C*, and to make it accessible to a broad learning and teaching community in modelling and simulation. The funding for this project will end by the end of 2023. It is planned to finish this work then.

Acknowledgement

This research was supported by „OpenEdu-RLP " [19] .

References

[1] J.Artal-Sevil, A. Gargallo, and M. Valero, "Flipped teaching and interactive tools. A multidisciplinary innovation experience in higher education." Sixth International Conference on Higher Education Advances, 2020, pp. 1–8.

[2] L. Zakfeld, S. Haag, and C. Simon, "Informal Ways to Educate About Formal Modeling and Simulation with Petri Nets," in *SIMUL 2022: The Fourteenth International Conference on Advances in System Simulation*, F. Herrmann, Ed., Lissabon (Portugal), 2022, pp. 38–43.

[3] P. Loos, R. Clarner, F. Hermann, T. Hess, A. Gadatsch, and E. Sinz, "Business and information systems engineering programs at universities and fachhochschulen – convergence or differentiation?" *Business & Information Systems Engineering*, vol. 5, pp. 281–286, 2013.

[4] German Accreditation Council, "System Accreditation," https://akkreditierungsrat.de/en/accreditation-system/system-accreditation/system-accreditation (last accessed 09.08.2023), 2023.

[5] Kultusministerkonferenz, "Qualifikationsrahmen für deutsche Hochschulabschlüsse," https://www.hrk.de/themen/studium/qualifikationsrahmen/ (last accessed 6.08.2023), 2017, German, transl. *Higher Qualifications Framework for German Higher Education Qualifications.*

[6] C. Simon, S. Haag, and L. Zakfeld, "The Process-Simulation.Center," in *SIM-SC: Special Track at SIMUL 2022: The Fourteenth International Conference on Advances in System Simulation*, F. Herrmann, Ed., Lissabon (Portugal), 2022, pp. 74–77.

[7] U. Ehlers, "Next Skills: Future Skills Finder," https://nextskills.org/future-skills-finder/ (last accessed 02.08.2023), 2023.

[8] G. Rivera et al., "Genetic algorithm for scheduling optimization considering heterogeneous containers: A real-world case study," *Axioms*, vol. 9, no. 1, pp. 27–43, 2020.

[9] P. Raju and C. Sankar, "Teaching Real-World Issues through Case Studies*," *Journal of Engineering Education*, vol. 88, no. 4, pp. 501–508, 1999.

[10] F. Gu, J. Guo, W. Zhang, P. A. Summers, and P. Hall, "From waste plastics to industrial raw materials: A life cycle assessment of mechanical plastic recycling practice based on a real-world case study," *Science of The Total Environment*, vol. 601-602, pp. 1192–1207, 2017.

[11] R. Mahmoudi and M. Rasti-Barzoki, "Sustainable supply chains under government intervention with a real-world case study: An evolutionary game theoretic approach," *Computers & Industrial Engineering*, vol. 116, pp. 130–143, 2018.

[12] C. Simon and S. Haag, "A Case-Study to Teach Process-Aware Information Systems," *EMISA Forum: Proceedings of the SIG Enterprise Modelling and Information Systems Architectures of the German Informatics Society*, vol. 40, pp. 9–10, 2020.

[13] L. Barnes, C. Christensen, and A. Hansen, *Teaching and the Case Method: Text, Cases, and Readings*, 3rd ed. Bosten: Harvard Business Review Press, 1994.

[14] Infraserv Logistics GmbH, "Overview hazardous substances warehouse," https://www.infraserv-logistics.com/en/isl/news/news/ (last accessed 15.08.2023), 2023.

[15] T. Bergs, S. Gierlings, T. Auerbach, A. Klink, D. Schraknepper, and T. Augspurger, "The Concept of Digital Twin and Digital Shadow in Manufacturing," *Procedia CIRP*, vol. 101, pp. 81–84, 2021, 9th CIRP Conference on High Performance Cutting.

[16] C. Simon, S. Haag, and L. Zakfeld, "Stratification of Timed Petri Nets at the Example of a Production Process," in *ECMS 2022: 36th International ECMS Conference on Modelling and Simulation*, 2022, pp. 128–134.

[17] S. Few, *Information Dashboard Design: Displaying Data for At-A-Glance Monitoring*, 1st ed. CA: Analytics Press, 2013.

[18] C. Simon, S. Haag, and L. Zakfeld, "Experiments on GPT-3 Assisted Process Model Development," in *ECMS 2023 : 37th International ECMS Conference on Modelling and Simulation*, Florenz (Italy), 2023, pp. 270–276.

[19] "OpenEdu-RLP," https://www.vcrp.de/projekte/oer-programm/ (last accessed 12.10.2023).

Crowdshipping with Dynamic Workers Availability – Restless-Bandit-Based Prioritization

Amin Karimi
School of Mathematics and Statistics
The University of Melbourne
Melbourne, Australia
Email: karimia@student.unimelb.edu.au

Jing Fu
School of Engineering
Royal Melbourne Institute of Technology
Melbourne, Australia
Email: jing.fu@rmit.edu.au

Lele Zhang
School of Mathematics and Statistics
The University of Melbourne
Melbourne, Australia
Email: lele.zhang@unimelb.edu.au

Hadi Ghaderi
School of Business, Law & Entrepreneurship
Swinburne University of Technology
Melbourne, Australia
Email: hghaderi@swin.edu.au

Abstract—**Exponential growth for last mile delivery demand has created several challenges for retailers and couriers, at the same time forcing the development of efficient and sustainable delivery solutions. One of the emerging solutions is crowd-sourced delivery, also known as crowdshipping. In a crowdshipping system, the general public participates in parcel delivery (known as crowdshippers) and then rewarded with remunerations. To develop sustainable and commercially viable crowdshipping solutions, capable of handling large-scale delivery tasks, effective assignment of tasks to crowdshippers is critical. Particularly when both tasks and crowdshippers dynamically arrive and depart the system, it becomes challenging to complete deliveries, while maximizing the total profit of the platform. This paper models the dynamic crowdshipping system using a Markov decision process and proposes a restless-bandit-based capacity relaxation technique to facilitate the task-to-crowdshipper assignment. Simulation results show that the proposed technique is superior over two baseline policies with respect to higher average profits and lower task rejection rates. The learning of this research provides important directions for the design and development of crowdshipping systems that are subject to both crowdshipper and task uncertainty.**

Index Terms—**stochastic process; restless bandits; crowdsourcing; task assignment; crowdshipping; parcel delivery**

I. Introduction

Fueled by exponential growth in e-commerce, more consumers are opting to purchase goods and services online [1]. This tendency has led to a surge in urban freight activity, particularly the Last Mile Delivery (LMD) of parcels to the doorstep of customers [2]. Furthermore, changing consumer expectations for fast, convenient and low-cost delivery options have forced retailers and logistics organizations to further expand their service configurations through increased coverage, frequency and speed, all of which lead to higher numbers of trips and vehicle activity in highly populated urban areas [3]. In tandem with these developments, efforts are being made to leverage digital technologies that could lead to efficient logistics operations, while minimizing negative environmental impacts [4]. One example of such advancements is the widespread use of mobile devices and app-based solutions that allow logistics works to be outsourced to individuals, also known as *crowd logistics* [5]. In the past decade, crowd logistics has received substantial momentum as an innovative solution that could potentially address some of the infrastructure and resource constraints of business logistics [6] [7]. In this paper, we study a form of crowd logistics service known as *crowdshipping (CS)*. Despite the absence of a uniform conceptualization, crowdshipping can be defined as a decentralized logistics system, in which individuals from the general public perform parcel delivery for an agreed compensation amount [8]. Predominantly, in such systems, the assignment of tasks to individuals, information sharing, and financial transactions are facilitated by a digital platform [9] [10].

Crowdshipping is inherently a complex and multifaceted problem that involves disciplines such as mathematics, computer science and transport engineering [11]. For example, the many-to-many nature of crowdshipping presents model complexity when considering the temporal and spatial considerations of delivery tasks and the pool of available *crowdshippers* [12]. Specifically, crowdshippers' mobility pattern is subject to constant variations. Second, crowdshipping relies on a pool of individuals who are connected via mobile devices that produce large mobility data, requiring sophisticated trajectory tools to understand and predict movement patterns [13]. Therefore, constant capturing and analyzing mobility data from a large number of individuals is computationally difficult. Third, the literature shows that crowdshippers are noticeably sensitive to their reimbursement [14] [15]. More specifically, crowdshipping platforms employ a wide range of people with varying compensation sensitivity. Therefore, a successful crowdshipping system should utilize compensation and pricing strategies that are fair to the crowd, yet, yield profit for the platform [16]. More specifically, higher compensations could attract more crowdshippers, while leaving little revenue for the platform. On the other hand, low compensation could discourage participation and eventually lead to lower revenue. Finally, relevant to the objective of this research, effectively assigning jobs to crowdshippers remains a key decision-making process to the long-term sustainability of crowdshipping platforms [17]. Optimized assignments could not only minimize operational costs by identifying the right crowd with lower compensation amounts, but they also have important implications for service quality (e.g., reliability, availability and speed) and customer retention [18]. For example, an effective task assignment mechanism is capable of identifying crowdshippers that are more aligned with the delivery task requirement, temporally and spatially, leading to a quicker and cost-effective process.

In light of the above considerations, we study a large-scale crowdshipping assignment problem with a long-run optimization objective, considering dynamic assignments of available and eligible crowdshippers to different delivery requests. In contrast to static optimization approaches that aim to maximize profit at one point in time, we aim to maximize average profit over a period of time with dynamic parameters. Specifically, we take into account the dynamic registration and de-registration of crowdshippers and the dynamic arrivals of delivery requests with various service levels. Such assumptions substantially complicate the formulation of the problem and prevent conventional optimization techniques from being applied here. We formulate the crowdshipping assignment problem as a stochastic system consisting of parallel bandit processes. In a special case with a fixed number of crowdshippers at all the time, the *Restless-Bandit-Based (RBB)* resource allocation technique studied in [19] leads to near-optimal results without consuming excessive computational power. However, for the general case with a dynamic crowdshippers pool, extended or new techniques are required. In this paper, we propose the *Restless-Bandit-Based Capacity Relaxation* (RBB-CR) technique to approximate the marginal profit of assigning an incoming delivery request to a registered crowdshipper. Then we develop and evaluate an assignment strategy, referred to as the RBB-CR policy, that always prioritizes the assignments of crowdshippers with the highest approximated marginal profits. Extensive numerical results demonstrate that the RBB-CR always outperforms two baseline policies with respect to the average revenue, cost, profit, and customer satisfaction. Such superiority is consistent for a variety of system sizes and loads. After a brief literature review in Section II, we explain the crowdshipping assignment problem and its model in Section III and then discuss strategies applied in Section IV. We discuss the settings and results of the numerical study in Section V, which is followed by a brief conclusion in Section VI.

II. Related Work

While the literature on crowdshipping has grown substantially in recent years, the task assignment remains a topical area among researchers [20]. Compared to the ride-sharing task assignment, where the temporal considerations of the trip are simplified by the traveler's origin and destination points, in crowdshipping both sender's and receiver's availability are subject to variations [21]. Similarly, delivery requests could arrive at an unknown pace, a feature comparable to passenger travel requests in ride-sharing systems [22]. On the supply side, many crowdshipping platforms rely on a pool of casual workers with varying temporal and spatial availability [8]. In other words, the properties of the crowdshippers pool vary dynamically in terms of size, temporal and spatial availability, but also their ability to move goods considering the weight and size [23].

Various modeling and solution techniques have been applied to solve the crowdshipping task assignment problems in mainly three settings, deterministic, dynamic and stochastic [17]. In the deterministic environment when all information is deterministic and available in advance, methods such as mixed-integer programming and benders decomposition are widely used to find the optimal assignment [24] [17]. Efforts have been made to study the stochasticity in crowdshippers' availability or willingness to deliver [25] [26]. For example, Mousavi et al. [25] developed a two-stage stochastic integer program and decomposition algorithms to match crowdshippers to delivery tasks and demonstrated the superiority of the stochastic approach over the deterministic. The crowdshipping system is essentially a dynamic system as delivery requests and crowdshippers dynamically arrive in and leave the system. Nevertheless, the literature on the dynamic crowdshipping problem is limited. Similarly, Ghaderi et al. [24] followed a mixed-integer programming approach, in which the objective was to maximize the profit of the platform by minimizing the reimbursement, while minimizing the trip detour required by crowdshippers to complete parcel delivery. In this work, authors relied on normal people accepting to deliver a parcel as part of their daily travels, therefore, relying on extensive trajectory analytics to understand mobility patterns for optimized task assignment. Farazi et al. [27] applied heuristics-embedded Deep Q-Network (DQN) algorithms to assign dynamically arriving requests to available crowdshippers. Agent-based simulations are another useful way to model the crowdshipping system as they can easily incorporate the dynamic arrivals and departures of delivery requests and resources as well as the intelligent, stochastic decision-making processes of crowdshippers [28]. Nevertheless, compared to the proposed approach, agent-based simulations would be limited by their convergence, scalability, transparency and interpretability.

III. A Crowdshipping Assignment Problem

Define $\mathbb{N}_+$ and $\mathbb{N}_0$ as the sets of positive and non-negative integers, respectively, and for any $N \in \mathbb{N}_+$, let $[N]$ represent the set $\{1, 2, \ldots, N\}$. Let $\mathbb{R}$, $\mathbb{R}_+$ and $\mathbb{R}_0$ be the sets of all, positive and non-negative real numbers, respectively.

Consider L different types of customers that are characterized by their origins (i.e., parcel collection points), destinations (i.e., delivery addresses), parcel sizes (weights and/or volumes), and other specific requirements of the delivery services (e.g., delivery urgency – same day, next day, etc.). The customers keep generating delivery requests to a crowdshipping system (platform) with various registered crowdshippers, also correspondingly classified into L types. Each delivery request may include multiple parcels. Crowdshippers are divided into M different classes based on their locations and eligibility of serving certain requests. For instance, big parcels can only be carried by crowdshippers equipped with vans or trucks; urgent parcels prefer nearby crowdshippers; and crowdshippers in different locations only agree to detour within certain geographical distances. For $\ell \in [L]$, let $\mathscr{M}_\ell$ represent the class set of crowdshippers that are eligible and willing to deliver parcels for type-ℓ requests.

When a delivery request arrives, an available crowdshipper will be selected to deliver the associated parcel(s); if there is no such crowdshipper, the delivery request will be *rejected*. In this research, crowdshippers are not allowed to decline the offer as long as they are available and eligible for a certain type of delivery task. While this could present a limitation for this study, at the same time, it allows for a higher level of service quality and system profitability. A crowdshipper may be able to serve more than one delivery request. We consider a *delivery weight*, $w_{\ell,m} \in [0,1]$, for a type-ℓ request matched with a class-m crowdshipper, meaning that the $w_{\ell,m}$ proportion of the crowdshipper's carrying capacity, such as vehicle's storage space, is used and occupied for the delivery request. For example, if a crowdshipper in class m is able to take three delivery requests of type ℓ, then we can set $w_{\ell,m} = \frac{1}{3}$ to formulate this case. In this case, the $w_{\ell,m}$ proportion of the crowdshipper's capacity is *occupied* and becomes *unavailable* for future requests until all the associated parcels are delivered. Upon successful delivery of a request, the crowdshipper becomes partially/fully *available* again to serve other requests. The crowdshippers dynamically join and leave the crowdshipping system, resulting in time-varying numbers of registered crowdshippers in each class. In other words, crowdshippers declare their availability for work randomly. Once a crowdshipper has been occupied by request(s), he or she will not leave the crowdshipping system until all the requests are fully completed.

Let $\bar{C}_m(t)$ represent the number of class-m crowdshippers that are assigned with some delivery requests at time t, and let $\bar{\boldsymbol{C}}(t) := (\bar{C}_m(t) : m \in [M])$. Furthermore, for $m \in [M]$, let $C_m(t)$ represent the total number of registered crowdshippers of class m in the system at time $t \geq 0$, which is affected by both people's willingness of becoming crowdshippers (i.e., signing up for crowdshipping) and the underlying strategies of matching them with different delivery requests. Formally, we define

$$C_m(t) := E_m(t) + \Delta_m(t), \tag{1}$$

where $E_m(t)$ is a random variable considered as a hyper-parameter reflecting people's willingness of staying in and joining the crowdshipping system at time t, and $\Delta_m(t) := \max\{0, \bar{C}_m(t) - E_m(t)\}$ is used to ensure that $C_m(t) \geq \bar{C}_m(t)$ all the time. In particular, $E_m(t)$ is bounded and takes values in $\mathbb{N}_+$. While some crowdshippers, who are on the way to deliver parcels, may wish to leave the system, causing $E_m(t) < \bar{C}_m(t)$ for some t, adding the second item $\Delta_m(t)$ in (1) aims to keep $C_m(t) = \bar{C}_m(t)$ when $E_m(t) < \bar{C}_m(t)$ so that these crowdshippers are required to finish their jobs before de-registration. Assume that $C_m(t)$ is observable all the time and is uniformly bounded for all $t \geq 0$. Let $\boldsymbol{C}(t) := (C_m(t) : m \in [M])$.

As mentioned in Section I, the long-run optimization problem proposed in this research is essential for operating a real-world crowdshipping system. Such an assumption significantly complicates the task assignment module and related analysis. To model the delivery requests with different types, we consider mean rates λ_ℓ ($\ell \in [L]$), each arriving with pre-determined origin, destination, parcel profiles, and some delivery preferences. Delivery time for each request is a random time that formulates uncertainties along the travel route. Request arrivals follow a Poisson distribution (see [29]). In Section V, extensive numerical results will be presented with time-variant Poisson arrivals that further capture the dynamic features of the system workloads in both busy and idle hours. For $\ell \in [L]$ and $m \in \mathscr{M}_\ell$, the duration of serving a type-ℓ request by a crowdshipper in class m is independently and identically distributed with mean $1/\mu_{\ell,m}$, where $\mu_{\ell,m} \in \mathbb{R}_+$. For $m \notin \mathscr{M}_\ell$, define $\mu_{\ell,m} \equiv 0$.

We make decisions upon the arrival of requests in an online manner without assuming given requests that will come in the future. Define $N_{\ell,m}(t)$ as the number of type-ℓ requests that are being served by a class-m crowdshipper at time t. Let $\boldsymbol{N}(t) := (N_{\ell,m}(t) : \ell \in [L], m \in [M])$, where $N_{\ell,m}(t) \equiv 0$ if $m \notin \mathscr{M}_\ell$. The number of occupied crowdshippers in class m at time t is given by $\bar{C}_m(t) = \sum_{\ell \in [L]} N_{\ell,m}(t) w_{\ell,m}$, which should not exceed the value of $C_m(t)$. More specifically, define $a_{\ell,m}(\boldsymbol{N}(t), \boldsymbol{C}(t)) \in \{0,1\}$ as an action variable indicating whether a type-ℓ request newly arrived at time t is going to be served by a crowdshipper in class m or not. If $a_{\ell,m}(\boldsymbol{N}(t), \boldsymbol{C}(t)) = 1$, the newly arrived type-ℓ request is served by a crowdshipper in class m; otherwise, not served by class-m crowdshippers. Define $a_{\ell,m}(\cdot,\cdot) \equiv 0$ if $m \notin \mathscr{M}_\ell$. The action variables are determined based on knowledge of $\boldsymbol{N}(t)$ and $\boldsymbol{C}(t)$ at time t and are subject to

$$\sum_{m \in \mathscr{M}_\ell \cup \{m_\ell\}} a_{\ell,m}(\boldsymbol{N}(t), \boldsymbol{C}(t)) = 1, \ \forall \ell \in [L], t \geq 0, \tag{2}$$

where m_ℓ is a dummy crowdshipper standing for rejection of a type-ℓ request, and

$$\sum_{\ell \in [L]} N_{\ell,m}(t) w_{\ell,m} + \sum_{\ell \in [L]} a_{\ell,m}(\boldsymbol{N}(t), \boldsymbol{C}(t)) w_{\ell,m} \leq C_m(t), \quad \forall m \in [M], t \geq 0. \tag{3}$$

In (2), for a newly arrived type-ℓ delivery request, we always select a crowdshipper to serve it or reject it - setting $a_{\ell,m_\ell}(\boldsymbol{N}(t), \boldsymbol{C}(t)) = 1$. Inequality (3) ensures that we only assign the registered crowdshippers to serve newly arrived delivery requests. In particular, upon a decision-making epoch t, we will check the number of registered crowdshippers. If

$C_m(t) = \bar{C}_m(t)$ at time t (i.e., all registered crowdshippers are occupied by earlier arrived parcels), then (3) enforces $a_{\ell,m}(\boldsymbol{N}(t), \boldsymbol{C}(t)) = 0$ for all $\ell \in [L]$. Unlike the canonical restless-bandit-based resource allocation problem discussed in [19], the right-hand side of constraint (3) (i.e., $C_m(t)$) is dependent on the employed crowdshipping assignment strategies. It prevents past results in [19], which assumes $C_m(t) \equiv C$ for some constant $C \in \mathbb{N}_+$, from being directly applied here.

Here, we adapt the RBB resource allocation technique in the request-crowdshipper assignment problem. More importantly, we extend the technique to practical scenarios with time-varying and strategy-dependent resource capacities. The stochastic process $\{(\boldsymbol{N}(t), \boldsymbol{C}(t)), t \geq 0\}$ evolves according to a transition kernel that is affected by the above-defined action variables $a_{\ell,m}(\boldsymbol{N}(t), \boldsymbol{C}(t))$ for all $\ell \in [L]$ and $m \in [M]$. Define a set Φ of crowdshipping assignment strategies determined by such action variables $a_{\ell,m}(\boldsymbol{N}(t), \boldsymbol{C}(t)) \in \{0, 1\}$. To emphasize the dependencies between the employed strategy, the action variables, and the underlying stochastic process, we rewrite $a_{\ell,m}(\cdot,\cdot)$, $\boldsymbol{N}(t)$, $\boldsymbol{C}(t)$ and $\bar{\boldsymbol{C}}(t)$ as $a^{\phi}_{\ell,m}(\cdot,\cdot)$, $\boldsymbol{N}^{\phi}(t)$, $\boldsymbol{C}^{\phi}(t)$ and $\bar{\boldsymbol{C}}^{\phi}(t)$ for $\phi \in \Phi$, respectively. We aim to maximize the long-run average profit of the crowdshipping system

$$\max_{\phi \in \Phi} \lim_{T \to +\infty} \frac{1}{T} \mathbb{E} \int_0^T \sum_{\ell \in [L]} \sum_{m \in [M]} R_{\ell,m}(N^{\phi}_{\ell,m}(t)) dt, \quad (4)$$

subject to (2) and (3), where $R_{\ell,m}(N^{\phi}_{\ell,m}(t))$ is the expected profit rate of the process $\{N^{\phi}_{\ell,m}(t), t \geq 0\}$. In particular, define the profit rate

$$R_{\ell,m}\left(N^{\phi}_{\ell,m}(t)\right) := p_{\ell} \mu_{\ell,m} N^{\phi}_{\ell,m}(t) - c_{\ell,m} N^{\phi}_{\ell,m}(t), \quad (5)$$

where p_{ℓ} is the monetary income of successfully delivering the parcel(s) for a request of type ℓ, $c_{\ell,m}$ is the cost rate per unit time per crowdshipper that is specified by the administration expenditure, the material and labor costs, etc., and $1/\mu_{\ell,m}$ is the expected delivery time for a class-m crowdshipper to complete the type-ℓ request. The product $\mu_{\ell,m} N^{\phi}_{\ell,m}(t)$ thus represents the expected number of type-ℓ requests completed by class-m crowdshippers per unit time at time t when the strategy ϕ is employed. We consider bounded $C_m(t)$ for all $m \in [M]$, hence the crowdshipping system is always stable with existing equilibrium average objective in the long-run regime. We refer to the problem described in (4), (2) and (3) as the *crowdshipping assignment problem* and also the *original problem*.

IV. Crowdshipping Assignment Strategies

The crowdshipping assignment problem is modeled by a Markov Decision Process (MDP) with state space

$$\mathscr{N} := \left(\prod_{\ell \in [L]} \prod_{m \in \mathscr{M}_{\ell}} \left\{0, 1, \ldots, \left\lfloor \frac{C}{w_{\ell,m}} \right\rfloor \right\} \right) \times \{0, 1, 2 \ldots, C\}^M$$

$$= \left(\prod_{\ell \in [L]} \prod_{m \in \mathscr{M}_{\ell}} \mathscr{N}_{\ell,m} \right) \times \{0, 1, 2 \ldots, C\}^M, \quad (6)$$

where $C \in \mathbb{N}_+$ is an upper bound of $C_m(t)$ for $m \in [M]$ satisfying $C \geq \max_{m \in [M]} C_m(t)$ for all $t \geq 0$, and $\mathscr{N}_{\ell,m} := \{0, 1, \ldots, \lceil C/w_{\ell,m} \rceil\}$. Observing that the crowdshipping assignment problem exhibits large state space that increases exponentially in the number of L and M. In general, an optimal solution is intractable for such problems, and conventional optimizers, including off-the-shelf reinforcement learning solutions, cannot be directly applied here due to the exposing state space.

We resort to near-optimal strategies that are applicable to large-scale systems without consuming excessive computational power. The RBB resource allocation technique in [19] proposes to approximate optimality by decomposing the high-dimensional MDP into $\sum_{\ell \in [L]} |\mathscr{M}_{\ell}|$ sub-processes, with each considered as an MDP with binary actions evolving within remarkably reduced state space. We refer to such sub-process as a *bandit process* that is associated with a request-crowdshipper (RCS) pair $(\ell, m) \in [L] \times [M]$. The marginal profit of selecting a class-m crowdshipper to serve a type-ℓ request is evaluated and quantified through a real number, whenever $N^{\phi}_{\ell,m}(t)$ and $C^{\phi}_m(t)$ are given. Following the tradition of the restless-bandit community, we refer to such real number as the *index* of the associated action of selecting a certain RCS pair, and, in each decision-making epoch, always prioritize the actions with the highest indices. The indices for each bandit process are computed independently from those of other bandit processes, which consume a limited amount of computational power and enable the applicability of the resulting crowdshipping strategy in the original problem (4), (2) and (3).

Since the crowdshipping problem studied here is complicated due to the strategy-dependent capacity $C^{\phi}_m(t)$ of crowdshipper resources, we approximate the marginal profits of selecting certain crowdshippers through appropriate randomization of the action variables and the capacities of crowdshippers in the asymptotic regime.

A. Restless-Bandit-Based Capacity Relaxation (RBB-CR)

Randomise the action variables and relax the constraints (2) and (3) to

$$\lim_{t \to +\infty} \sum_{m \in \mathscr{M}_{\ell} \cup \{m_{\ell}\}} \mathbb{E}\left[a^{\phi}_{\ell,m}(\boldsymbol{N}(t), \boldsymbol{C}(t))\right] = 1, \forall \ell \in [L], \quad (7)$$

and

$$\lim_{t \to +\infty} \sum_{\ell \in [L]} w_{\ell,m} \mathbb{E}\left[N^{\phi}_{\ell,m}(t)\right] + \lim_{t \to +\infty} \sum_{\ell \in [L]} w_{\ell,m} \mathbb{E}\left[a^{\phi}_{\ell,m}(\boldsymbol{N}^{\phi}(t), \boldsymbol{C}^{\phi}(t))\right] \leq \lim_{t \to +\infty} \sum_{\ell \in [L]} w_{\ell,m} \mathbb{E}\left[C^{\phi}_m(t)\right], \forall m \in [M], \quad (8)$$

respectively. We note that in a stable system, for a given strategy ϕ, the steady-state distributions of the random variables $\boldsymbol{N}^{\phi}(t)$ and $\boldsymbol{C}^{\phi}(t)$ exist as $t \to +\infty$. Define a set $\tilde{\Phi}$ of all crowdshipping strategies that are determined by the randomized action variables, and consider a relaxed version of the crowdshipping assignment problem

$$\max_{\phi\in\tilde{\Phi}} \lim_{T\to+\infty} \frac{1}{T}\mathbb{E}\int_0^T \sum_{\ell\in[L]}\sum_{m\in[M]} R_{\ell,m}(N^{\phi}_{\ell,m}(t))dt, \quad (9)$$

which achieves an upper bound to the maximum of the original crowdshipping assignment problem. We refer to the problem described in (9), (7) and (8) as the *relaxed problem*.

Consider a strategy $\phi^* \in \tilde{\Phi}$ that is optimal to the relaxed problem described in (9), (7) and (8). Based on the existence of the steady-state distributions, there exists the limit $C^*_m = \lim_{t\to+\infty}\mathbb{E}\big[\bar{\boldsymbol{C}}^{\phi^*}_m(t)\big]$. We construct a *surrogate* version of the relaxed problem by replacing the constraints in (8) with

$$\lim_{t\to+\infty}\sum_{\ell\in[L]} w_{\ell,m}\mathbb{E}\Big[N^{\phi}_{\ell,m}(t)\Big] + \lim_{t\to+\infty}\sum_{\ell\in[L]} w_{\ell,m}\mathbb{E}\Big[a^{\phi}_{\ell,m}(\boldsymbol{N}^{\phi}(t),\boldsymbol{C}^{\phi}(t))\Big] \leq C^*_m, \forall m\in[M], \quad (10)$$

We refer to the problem described by (9), (7) and (10) as the *surrogate problem*. The strategy ϕ^* satisfies (7) and (10) and thus is also applicable to the surrogate problem. It follows that the maximum of the surrogate problem achieves an upper bound to that of the relaxed problem and the original crowdshipping assignment problem.

For $\ell\in[L]$ and $m\in[M]$, define

$$\alpha^{\phi}_{\ell,m}(n,c) := \lim_{t\to+\infty}\mathbb{E}\Big[a^{\phi}_{\ell,m}(\boldsymbol{N}^{\phi}(t),\boldsymbol{C}^{\phi}(t)) \Big| N^{\phi}_{\ell,m}(t)=n, C^{\phi}_m(t)=c\Big], \quad (11)$$

which takes values in $[0,1]$. From [19, Proposition 4], there exist an optimal solution $\tilde{\phi}\in\tilde{\Phi}$ for the surrogate problem, $\boldsymbol{\nu}\in\mathbb{R}^L$ and $\boldsymbol{\gamma}\in\mathbb{R}^M_0$ such that, for $\ell\in[L]$, $m\in\mathscr{M}_\ell\cup\{m_\ell\}$ and $(n,c)\in\mathscr{N}_{\ell,m}\times\{0,1,\ldots,C\}$, if

$$\nu_\ell < \frac{\lambda_\ell}{\mu_{\ell,m}}R_{\ell,m}(n) - (1+\frac{\lambda_\ell}{\mu_{\ell,m}})w_{\ell,m}\gamma_m, \quad (12)$$

then $\alpha^{\tilde{\phi}}_{\ell,m}(n,c)=1$; if

$$\nu_\ell = \frac{\lambda_\ell}{\mu_{\ell,m}}R_{\ell,m}(n) - (1+\frac{\lambda_\ell}{\mu_{\ell,m}})w_{\ell,m}\gamma_m, \quad (13)$$

then $\alpha^{\tilde{\phi}}_{\ell,m}(n,c)=a$ where $a\in[0,1]$; otherwise, $\alpha^{\tilde{\phi}}_{\ell,m}(n,c)=0$. Note that, in (12) and (13), the value of $\alpha^{\tilde{\phi}}_{\ell,m}(n,c)$ is independent from c.

More importantly, such strategy $\tilde{\phi}$ can be constructed without assuming any knowledge of $\boldsymbol{\nu}$, $\boldsymbol{\gamma}$ and C^*_m. Define a ranking $\mathscr{o}$ of the RCS-State (RCSS) tuples $(\ell,m,n)\in\prod_{\ell\in[L]}\prod_{m\in\mathscr{M}_\ell\cup\{m_\ell\}}\mathscr{N}_{\ell,m}$ that are ranked according to the descending order of

$$\eta_{\ell,m}(n) := \frac{\frac{\lambda_\ell}{\mu_{\ell,m}}R_{\ell,m}(n)}{w_{\ell,m}(1+\frac{\lambda_\ell}{\mu_{\ell,m}})}, \quad (14)$$

where $\eta_{\ell,m_\ell}(n)\equiv 0$. For $(\ell,m)\in\prod_{\ell\in[L]}\mathscr{M}_\ell\cup\{m_\ell\}$, if $\eta_{\ell,m}(n)=\eta_{\ell,m}(n')$ with $n<n'$, then the tuple (ℓ,m,n) precedes (ℓ,m,n'). Other tie cases are broken arbitrarily. Let $\boldsymbol{\eta} := (\eta_{\ell,m}(n) : \ell\in[L], m\in\mathscr{M}_\ell\cup\{m_\ell\}, n\in\mathscr{N}_{\ell,m})$. Given $\mathscr{o}$, the strategy $\tilde{\phi}$ can be determined by plugging the ranking $\mathscr{o}$ in [19, Algorithm 1]. Since the policy $\tilde{\phi}$ is optimal to the surrogate problem, it achieves an upper bound of the maximum of the original crowdshipping assignment problem, which is the main concern of this paper. In general, $\tilde{\phi}$ is not applicable to the original problem because it does not necessarily satisfy (2) and (3). Nonetheless, the priority style of $\tilde{\phi}$ reveals and quantifies the importance of selecting certain RCS pairs through the $\boldsymbol{\eta}$-based tuple ranking $\mathscr{o}$.

Input : Indices $\boldsymbol{\eta}$ and the state variables $(\boldsymbol{N}^{\text{RBB-CR}}(t), \boldsymbol{C}^{\text{RBB-CR}}(t))$ at time t.
Output: $\boldsymbol{a}^{\text{RBB-CR}}(\boldsymbol{N}^{\text{RBB-CR}}(t), \boldsymbol{C}^{\text{RBB-CR}}(t))$
Function *RBB-CR*
  $\boldsymbol{a}^{\text{RBB-CR}}(\boldsymbol{N}^{\text{RBB-CR}}(t), \boldsymbol{C}^{\text{RBB-CR}}(t)) \leftarrow \boldsymbol{0}$, $\boldsymbol{q}\leftarrow 0$
  Initialise a set $\mathscr{A}$ of all the RCSS tuples $(\ell,m,n)\in\prod_{\ell\in[L]}\prod_{m\in\mathscr{M}_\ell\cup\{m_\ell\}}\mathscr{N}_{\ell,m}$ with $N^{\text{RBB-CR}}_{\ell,m}(t)=n$.
  Build a maximum heap $\mathscr{H}$ of the set $\mathscr{A}$ according to the descending order of the RBB-CR indices.
  while $\mathscr{H}\neq\emptyset$ **do**
    $(\ell,m,n)\leftarrow$ the root node of the maximum heap $\mathscr{H}$
    if $q_\ell=0$ *and the constraints in* (2) *and* (3) *are not violated by setting* ϕ *=RBB-CR and* $a^{\text{RBB-CR}}_{\ell,m}(n)=1$ **then**
      $a^{\text{RBB-CR}}_{\ell,m}(\boldsymbol{N}^{\text{RBB-CR}}(t), \boldsymbol{C}^{\text{RBB-CR}}(t))\leftarrow 1$
      $q_\ell\leftarrow 1$
    end
    $\mathscr{H}$ pops the root node
  end
  return $\boldsymbol{a}^{\text{RBB-CR}}(\boldsymbol{N}^{\text{RBB-CR}}(t), \boldsymbol{C}^{\text{RBB-CR}}(t))$
End

Fig. 1: Pseudo-code for implementing the RBB-CR policy.

B. Restless-Bandit-Based (RBB) Crowdshipping Policy

Intuitively, the policy $\tilde{\phi}$ (optimal to the surrogate problem) always prioritizes the tuples with higher $\eta_{\ell,m}(n)$, which represents the marginal profit of its associated action - selecting a crowdshipper in class m to serve a delivery request of type ℓ when $N^{\phi}_{\ell,m}(t)=n$. Although $\eta_{\ell,m}(n)$ exists in a closed form, it considers the past and future profits of the process $\{N^{\phi}_{\ell,m}(t), t\geq 0\}$ that are possibly gained by taking the associated selection. Following the tradition of the restless bandit problems, we refer to $\eta_{\ell,m}(n)$ as the *restless-bandit-based capacity relaxation (RBB-CR) index* of the bandit process $\{N^{\phi}_{\ell,m}(t), t\geq 0\}$ when $N^{\phi}_{\ell,m}(t)=n$.

Following the form of $\tilde{\phi}$ and the RBB resource allocation technique in [19], we propose a crowdshipping assignment strategy, applicable to the original problem described in (4), (2) and (3), by prioritizing selections of RCS pairs (ℓ,m) (selecting a crowdshipper in class m to serve a delivery request of type ℓ) according to the descending order of the RBB-CR indices $\boldsymbol{\eta}$. We refer to such crowdshipping assignment strategy as the RBB-CR policy.

At time $t \geq 0$, we observe the variables $\boldsymbol{N}^{\text{RBB-CR}}(t)$ and $\boldsymbol{C}^{\text{RBB-CR}}(t)$ and determine the action variables

$$\boldsymbol{a}^{\text{RBB-CR}}\big(\boldsymbol{N}^{\text{RBB-CR}}(t), \boldsymbol{C}^{\text{RBB-CR}}(t)\big) := \Big(a^{\text{RBB-CR}}_{\ell,m}\big(\boldsymbol{N}^{\text{RBB-CR}}(t), \boldsymbol{C}^{\text{RBB-CR}}(t)\big) : \ell \in [L], m \in \mathscr{M}_\ell \cup \{m_\ell\}\Big) \quad (15)$$

in the steps described in Fig. 1. In particular, we start with initializing $\boldsymbol{a}^{\text{RBB-CR}}\big(\boldsymbol{N}^{\text{RBB-CR}}(t), \boldsymbol{C}^{\text{RBB-CR}}(t)\big)$ to be $\mathbf{0}$, a vector set $\boldsymbol{q} \in \{0,1\}^L$ to be $\mathbf{0}$, and a set $\mathscr{A}$ of all the RCSS tuples $(\ell, m, n) \in \prod_{\ell\in[L]} \prod_{m\in\mathscr{M}_\ell\cup\{m_\ell\}} \mathscr{N}_{\ell,m}$ with $N^{\text{RBB-CR}}_{\ell,m}(t) = n$. All the tuples in $\mathscr{A}$ are ranked according to the descending order of their RBB-CR indices, where tie cases are broken by selecting smaller $N^{\text{RBB-CR}}_{\ell,m}(t)$. Let $(\ell_\iota, m_\iota, n_\iota)$ represent the ιth tuple in $\mathscr{A}$, where $\iota = 1, 2, \ldots, |\mathscr{A}|$. In Lines 5 to 11 of the RBB-CR policy in Fig. 1, we seek for the smallest $\iota \in [|\mathscr{A}|]$ such that $q_{\ell_\iota} = 0$ and the constraints in (2) and (3) are not violated by setting ϕ = RBB-CR and $a^{\text{RBB-CR}}_{\ell_\iota,m_\iota}\big(\boldsymbol{N}^{\text{RBB-CR}}(t), \boldsymbol{C}^{\text{RBB-CR}}(t)\big) = 1$. For this smallest ι complying with (2) and (3), set $a^{\text{RBB-CR}}_{\ell_\iota,m_\iota}\big(\boldsymbol{N}^{\text{RBB-CR}}(t), \boldsymbol{C}^{\text{RBB-CR}}(t)\big) = 1$, $q_{\ell_\iota} = 1$, and keep exploring the remaining elements in $\mathscr{A}$ (exploring larger $\iota \in [|\mathscr{A}|]$). Including ordering of the RCSS tuples in $\mathscr{A}$, the computational complexity of the RBB-CR policy in Fig. 1 is $O(LM\log(LM))$, which is fast for large L and M. Upon an arrival of a delivery request of type $\ell \in [L]$, we assign a crowdshipper in the class $m \in \mathscr{M}_\ell$ with $a^{\text{RBB-CR}}_{\ell,m}\big(\boldsymbol{N}^{\text{RBB-CR}}(t), \boldsymbol{C}^{\text{RBB-CR}}(t)\big) = 1$ or reject it.

In the unrealistic case with constant $C^\phi_m(t) \equiv C$ for all $m \in [M]$, from [19, Theorem EC.1], the underlying stochastic process under the RBB-CR policy converges to a fixed point, referred to as the *global attractor*, *almost surely* as the number of crowdshippers and the arrival rates of delivery requests tend to infinity, proportionately. It follows that the RBB-CR coincides with the policy $\tilde{\phi}$ in the asymptotic regime. More specifically, RBB-CR is *asymptotically optimal* to the crowdshipping assignment problem described in (4), (2) and (3) as the number of crowdshippers and the arrival rates of delivery requests tend to infinity proportionately.

We argue that the global attractor still exists in the case with the strategy-dependent $C^\phi_m(t)$. Observing that RBB-CR is independent of the exact values of C^*_m for $m \in [M]$, we can replace C^*_m in (10) with $\lim_{t\to+\infty} \mathbb{E}\big[C^{\text{RBB-CR}}_m(t)\big]$, and it will lead to the same RBB-CR indices and a priority style policy, similar to $\tilde{\phi}$ and denoted by $\tilde{\varphi}$, achieving an upper bound of the original maximization problem. When the number of crowdshippers and the arrival rates of the delivery requests increase proportionately to a parameter $h \to +\infty$ (i.e., approach the asymptotic regime with the *scaling parameter* h), the transition rates of the underlying process $\{\boldsymbol{N}^{\text{RBB-CR}}(t), \boldsymbol{C}^{\text{RBB-CR}}(t), t \geq 0\}$ will also increase correspondingly. The normalized state vector $\big(\boldsymbol{N}^{\text{RBB-CR}}(t)/h, \boldsymbol{C}^{\text{RBB-CR}}(t)/h\big)$ is likely to stay in a neighborhood of a fixed point as $h \to +\infty$, similar to the case with $C^\phi_m(t) \equiv C$, leading to the asymptotic optimality of the RBB-CR policy.

V. Numerical Results

This section is devoted to evaluating the performance of the proposed RBB-CR policy through some numerical experiments.

A. Simulation Settings

Consider $M = 10$ different classes of crowdshippers. The crowdshippers are distinguished by their transport modes: with and without vehicles. If crowdshippers in the class $m \in [M]$ of crowdshippers have no vehicles, then we normalize the moving speed v_m to be 1, if they have no vehicles and adopt other transport modes (e.g., public transport, bikes or e-bikes); otherwise, set the moving speed to be $v_m = 2.5$. Each crowdshipper class $m \in [M]$ corresponds to a geographical region with the *geographical center* (x_m, y_m), and the crowdshippers in the class are randomly distributed in this region with the location denoted by a random vector $(X_m, Y_m) \in \mathbb{R}_0 \times \mathbb{R}_0$ with the mean $(x_m, y_m) = (\mathbb{E}X_m, \mathbb{E}Y_m)$. The geographical centers are randomly distributed in a 2-D plane $[0, 50] \times [0, 50]$.

For class $m \in [M]$, the cost rates (per unit time) $c_{\ell,m}$ for the crowdshipping system to hire the crowdshippers to serve an ℓ-request are set to be $\bar{c}_m \in \mathbb{R}_+$ for all $\ell \in [L]$. If the crowdshippers of class $m \in [M]$ deliver parcels with vehicles, then $\bar{c}_m$ is uniformly randomly generated from $[5, 10]$; otherwise, uniformly randomly taken from $[0.1, 3]$.

For each class $m \in [M]$, the number of crowdshippers that are willing to stay in the system at time t, $E_m(t)$, is set to $\lceil \max\{0, \bar{E}_m + \Delta_m(t)\}\rceil$, where $\bar{E}_m \in \mathbb{R}_+$ is uniformly randomly generated from $[5, 10]$, and $\Delta_m(t) \in \mathbb{R}$ is a normally distributed random number at time t. In Section V-C, we will explore the performance of systems with increasing $\bar{E}_m$ and compatibly many delivery requests per unit time.

In this preliminary numerical study, we consider $L = 2$ types of delivery requests: urgent (type $\ell = 1$) and regular (type $\ell = 2$) delivery. The proposed model scales well and can easily handle large L without consuming significantly more computational expenses. The monetary incomes p_1 and p_2 of completing delivery requests of the two types are uniformly distributed in $[200, 300]$ and $[100, 150]$, respectively. The delivery requests of type $\ell \in [L]$ keep arriving in the system with rates λ_ℓ that are randomly generated from $[1, 1.5]$. The origin position of an ℓ-request is randomly deployed in a region of the 2-D plane with expectation $(\bar{x}_\ell, \bar{y}_\ell) \in [0, 50] \times [0, 50]$. The deliver distance for a crowdshipper of class $m \in [M]$ to deliver the ℓ-request is set to $D_\ell = v_m \cdot \frac{1}{\mu_{\ell,m}}$, where v_m is the moving speed of the class-m crowdshippers and $\mu_{\ell,m}$ is the reciprocal of the expected time used to deliver a parcel from its origin position. For $\ell \in [L]$, consider $d_\ell = \mathbb{E}D_\ell = \lambda_\ell/\rho$, where $\rho \in \mathbb{R}_+$ is a given parameter representing the offered traffic intensity of the system. We adjust different values for ρ, indicating regular and busy periods of the crowdshipping system, in the following simulations. In this context, the total cost for a crowdshipper of class m to deliver an ℓ-parcel is equal to the cost rate $c_{\ell,m}$ multiplying the delivery time $\frac{D_\ell}{v_m}$.

For ℓ-requests, the eligibility of crowdshippers is based on

- the distance between the origin location of the parcel and the geographical center of the crowdshippers; and
- the relationship between the delivery type and the working modes of the crowdshippers.

In particular, urgent delivery requests can only be served by crowdshippers with vehicles while regular requests can be served by crowdshippers in either working mode. The exact settings of the eligibility between different requests and crowdshippers, specified as $\mathscr{M}_\ell$ ($\ell \in [L]$), are provided in Appendix A, together with the instance values of all the above mentioned random variables for the simulations. The model was coded using the C++ language and implemented on the high performance computing platform, Spartan [30], offered by The University of Melbourne.

B. Performance Evaluation

We demonstrate the effectiveness of the RBB-CR policy by comparing it to two baselines policies: Highest-Price (HP) and Shortest-Distance (SD). The HP and SD policies are greedy policies that always prioritize RCS pairs (ℓ, m) with the highest monetary incomes p_ℓ and the shortest travel distances, respectively. The travel distance for an RCS pair (ℓ, m) is defined as the sum of the expected delivery distance and the distance between the geographical center (x_m, y_m) of the crowdshipper class and the mean origin $(\bar{x}_\ell, \bar{y}_\ell)$ of the ℓ-requests. Tie cases are broken by selecting smaller $N^\phi_{\ell,m}(t)$ for $\phi =$HP and SD. The HP and SD policies are constructed through the same steps as RBB-CR (with pseudo-code provided in Fig. 1) except that the RCS pairs (ℓ, m) should be ranked according to the descending order of the monetary incomes p_ℓ and the ascending order of the travel distances, respectively.

In Fig. 2, we demonstrate the effectiveness of the three policies, with respect to the average revenue, average cost, average profit, and rejection rate, against the time horizon, when $\rho = 5$. More precisely, the average revenue and average cost of a policy $\phi \in \Phi$ with time horizon $T \in \mathbb{R}_+$ are

$$\mathfrak{R}^\phi_T := \frac{1}{T}\mathbb{E}\int_0^T \sum_{\ell\in[L]} \sum_{m\in[M]} p_\ell \mu_{\ell,m} N^\phi_{\ell,m}(t)dt, \tag{16}$$

and

$$\mathfrak{C}^\phi_T := \frac{1}{T}\mathbb{E}\int_0^T \sum_{\ell\in[L]} \sum_{m\in[M]} c_{\ell,m} N^\phi_{\ell,m}(t)dt, \tag{17}$$

respectively. The revenue $\mathfrak{R}^\phi_T$ is the amount of money that the crowdshipping platform receives from the senders for successfully delivering parcels, while the cost is what the platform pays the crowdshippers for performing deliveries until time T. The average profit $\mathfrak{P}^\phi_T$ is defined as the difference $\mathfrak{R}^\phi_T - \mathfrak{C}^\phi_T$. The rejection rate $\mathfrak{J}^\phi_T$ is the ratio of the number of rejected requests to the total under the policy ϕ during the time period $[0, T]$. It is an indicator of customer dissatisfaction; a higher rejection rate implies more rejected requests and lower customer satisfaction. The objective function in (4) is equal to $\lim_{T\to+\infty} \mathfrak{P}^\phi_T$.

In Fig. 2, RBB-CR always outperforms all the other policies, and the performance quickly becomes stable as T increases; that is, $\mathfrak{P}^{\text{RBB-CR}}_T$ is already close to its long-run average profit for relatively small T. RBB-CR achieves significantly better performance with respect to the four criteria. In particular, it achieves over 25% higher average profits compared to the other policies, implying its effectiveness with respect to the crowdshipping assignment problem described in (4), (2) and (3).

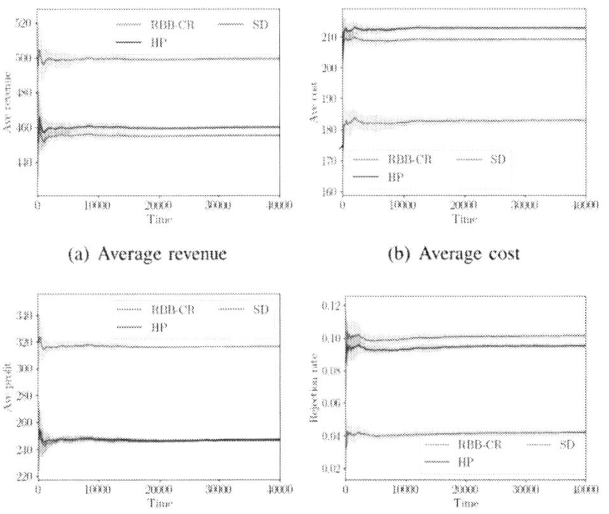

(a) Average revenue (b) Average cost

(c) Average profit (d) Average rejection rate

Fig. 2: Performance measures under different policies against time horizon, where the error bars are the standard deviations.

C. Performance Evaluation in Scaled Systems

Consider a *scaling parameter* $h \in \mathbb{N}_+$. For class $m \in [M]$, re-consider the number of crowdshippers willing to stay at time t and the arrival rates as $E_m(t) = h\bar{E}^0_m + \Delta_m(t)$ and $\lambda_m = h\lambda^0_m$, respectively, where $\bar{E}^0_m, \lambda^0_m \in \mathbb{R}_+$ are given parameters set equal to $\bar{E}_m$ and λ_m for the simulations discussed in Section V-B. All the other system parameters remain unchanged as those for Section V-B. In this context, we can scale the size of the crowdshipping system with compatibly many delivery requests through h. We refer to such a crowdshipping system scaled with parameter h as the *scaled system*, and the system discussed in Section V-B is a special case with $h = 1$.

In Fig. 3, we compare the long-run average profits normalized by the scaling parameter h (that is, $\lim_{T\to+\infty} \mathfrak{P}^\phi_T/h$) under the three policies $\phi =$RBB-CR, HP, and SD for $\rho = 5$ and 8, respectively. Similarly, in Fig. 4, we present the long-run average rejection rates of all the policies for both offered traffic intensities. From the definition, higher ρ implies longer delivery distances for the parcels and a heavier workload for

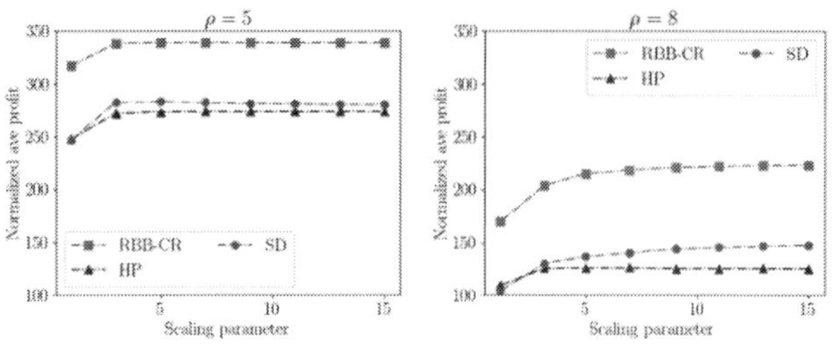

(a) (b)

Fig. 3: Normalized profits under different policies against the scaling parameter: (a) $\rho = 5$; and (b) $\rho = 8$.

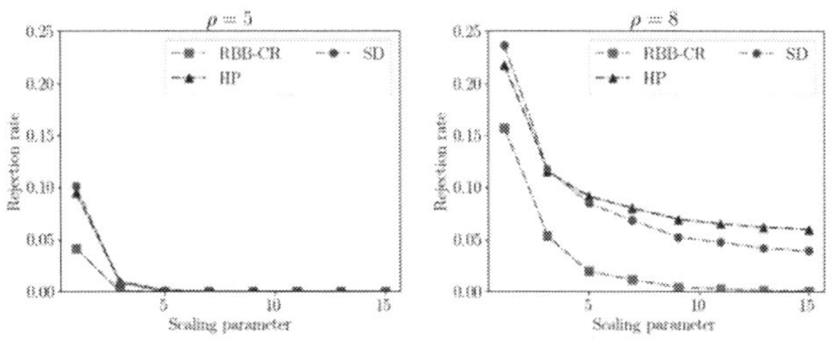

(a) (b)

Fig. 4: Rejection rates under different policies against the scaling parameter: (a) $\rho = 5$; and (b) $\rho = 8$.

the crowdshipping system. The higher delivery distances lead to higher costs and lower profits, and the heavier workload means higher probabilities of rejecting arriving requests, which is consistent with the observations in Figures 3 and 4.

In Figs. 3(b) and 4(b), the normalized average profit and the rejection rate of RBB-CR becomes relatively stable as the scaling parameter h increases. In particular, the rejection rate significantly decreases as h increments from 1 to 10 and maintains almost no change when $h \geq 10$. The normalized profit of RBB-CR in Figs. 3(b) varies similarly with increasing h. It implies that the underlying stochastic system $N^{\text{RBB-CR}}(t)$ has already reached the neighborhood of a stable point–it has already been close to its asymptotic behavior–when h is relatively small. In Figs. 3 and 4, RBB-CR maintains its clear advantages against all the tested baseline policies with respect to both the long-run average profit and the rejection rate.

VI. Conclusions

Effective task assignment is essential for the long-term sustainability of crowdshipping systems. While the extant body of the literature demonstrates several works aiming to maximize the profit of crowdshipping systems [24] [31] [32], they are mainly focused on a point in time. In other words, real-time assignment for profit maximization remains an area for further research. In this paper, we proposed a restless-bandit-based capacity relaxation technique to approximate the marginal profit of the crowdshipping system. We further developed a task assignment strategy, referred to as the RBB-CR policy, that prioritizes the assignment of work to crowdshippers that yield to highest approximated marginal profits. This technique allows for maximizing profits of large-scale crowdshipping problems in real time. Furthermore, we note that most crowdshipping systems consider a single type of delivery. The model proposed in this work accommodates multiple types of deliveries, which brings additional complexity to the model and computation.

To evaluate the performance of the proposed RBB-CR approach, we tested performance indicators of average revenue, cost, profit, and rejection rate, against two baseline greedy policies that prioritize the highest reimbursement and shortest travel distance. Our experimental results demonstrate that the RBB-CR policy outperforms two baseline policies, Highest Price and Shortest Distance, in some cases resulting in 25% higher average profit for the crowdshipping platform. In large-scale testing, similarly, the RBB-CR policy outperforms other baseline policies in terms of long-run average profit and the rejection rate. This performance is attributed to the unique mechanism of RBB-CR to approximate the marginal profit of assigning incoming delivery tasks to available crowdshippers.

Our work also comes with limitations that provide directions for future research. In this research, once the platform assigns a task to crowdshippers, they are not allowed to decline it. Such a feature is not commonly practized in modern crowd logistics systems. This limitation could significantly hinder the willingness of crowdshippers to participate in the system. Therefore, we suggest future research to incorporate task rejection into the model and policy design and further examine how such features could impact profitability and service quality. This consideration could also examine whether higher compensation rates could offset the non-rejection restriction.

Appendix A
Simulation Parameters

For the simulations presented in this paper, as described in Section V-A, we take instances of the random variables for the system parameters. In particular,

- $v_1 = 1$, $(x_1, y_1) = (27.00, 47.67)$, $\bar{E}_1 = 5.48$, and $\bar{c}_1 = 0.47$;
- $v_2 = 2.5$, $(x_2, y_2) = (12.97, 38.87)$, $\bar{E}_2 = 5.83$, and $\bar{c}_2 = 8.82$;
- $v_3 = 2.5$, $(x_3, y_3) = (30.17, 41.09)$, $\bar{E}_3 = 9.64$, and $\bar{c}_3 = 8.82$;
- $v_4 = 1$, $(x_4, y_4) = (46.79, 34.25)$, $\bar{E}_4 = 9.25$, and $\bar{c}_4 = 0.47$;
- $v_5 = 1$, $(x_5, y_5) = (16.93, 19.47)$, $\bar{E}_5 = 7.13$, and $\bar{c}_5 = 0.47$;
- $v_6 = 2.5$, $(x_6, y_6) = (7.38, 42.54)$, $\bar{E}_6 = 8.23$, and $\bar{c}_6 = 8.82$;
- $v_7 = 2.5$, $(x_7, y_7) = (9.78, 30.39)$, $\bar{E}_7 = 9.53$, and $\bar{c}_7 = 8.82$;
- $v_8 = 1$, $(x_8, y_8) = (42.71, 1.42)$, $\bar{E}_8 = 5.15$, and $\bar{c}_8 = 0.47$;
- $v_9 = 1$, $(x_9, y_9) = (9.41, 17.13)$, $\bar{E}_9 = 9.33$, and $\bar{c}_9 = 0.47$;

- and $v_{10} = 2.5$, $(x_{10}, y_{10}) = (24.92, 31.34)$, $\bar{E}_{10} = 9.63$, and $\bar{c}_{10} = 8.82$.

The urgent delivery request (type-1 requests) have $\lambda_1 = 1.49$, $p_1 = 276.34$, $w_{1,m} = 4.25$ for all $m \in \mathscr{M}_1$, $(\bar{x}_1, \bar{y}_1) = (7.38, 42.54)$, and $\mathscr{M}_1 = \{2, 3, 6, 7, 10\}$; and, for the regular requests (type-2 requests), we set $\lambda_2 = 1.17$, $p_2 = 101.36$, $w_{2,m} = 1.56$ for all $m \in \mathscr{M}_2$, $(\bar{x}_1, \bar{y}_1) = (30.17, 41.09)$, and $\mathscr{M}_2 = \{1, 2, 3, 4, 6, 7, 10\}$. Recall that, as described in Section V-A, all the above listed numbers are instances of pseudo-random numbers.

REFERENCES

[1] A. Risberg. and H. Jafari, "Last mile practices in e-commerce: framework development and empirical analysis of swedish firms," *International Journal of Retail & Distribution Managemen*, vol. 50, no. 8/9, pp. 942–961, 2022.

[2] A. Pahwa and M. Jaller, "Assessing last-mile distribution resilience under demand disruptions," *Transportation Research Part E: Logistics & Transportation Review*, vol. 172, p. 103066, 2023.

[3] S. Pan, L. Zhang, R. G. Thompson, and H. Ghaderi, "parcel network flow approach for joint delivery networks using parcel lockers," *International Journal of Production Research*, vol. 59, no. 7, pp. 2090–2115, 2021.

[4] S. Wicaksono, X. Lin, and L. Tavasszy, "Market potential of bicycle crowdshipping: A two-sided acceptance analysis," *Research in Transportation Business & Management*, vol. 45, no. Part A, p. 100660, 2022.

[5] H. Buldeo Rai, S. Verlinde, J. Merckx, and C. Macharis, "Crowd logistics: an opportunity for more sustainable urban freight transport?" *European Transport Research Review*, vol. 9, no. 3, pp. 1–13, 2017.

[6] A. Alnaggar, F. Gzara, and J. Bookbinder, "Crowdsourced delivery: A review of platforms and academic literature," *Omega*, vol. 98, p. 102139, 2021.

[7] A. Fessler, M. Thorhauge, S. Mabit, and S. Haustein, ". a public transport-based crowdshipping concept as a sustainable last-mile solution: Assessing user preferences with a stated choice experiment," *Transportation Research Part A: Policy and Practice*, vol. 158, pp. 210–223, 2020.

[8] H. Ghaderi, L. Zhang, P. Tsai, and J. Woo, "Crowdsourced last-mile delivery with parcel lockers," *International Journal of Production Economics*, vol. 251, p. 108549, 2022.

[9] A. Punel and A. Stathopoulos, "Modeling the acceptability of crowdsourced goods deliveries: Role of context and experience effects," *Transportation Research Part E: Logistics and Transportation Review*, vol. 105, pp. 518–38, 2017.

[10] V. Castillo, D. Mollenkopf, J. Bell, and T. Esper, "Designing technology for on-demand delivery: The effect of customer tipping on crowdsourced driver behavior and last mile performance," *Journal of Operations Management*, vol. 68, pp. 424–453, 2022.

[11] S. S. Mohri, H. Ghaderi, N. Nassir, and R. Thompson, "Crowdshipping for sustainable urban logistics: A systematic review of the literature," *Transportation Research Part E: Logistics and Transportation Review*, p. 178, 2023.

[12] M. Behrend, F. Meisel, K. Fagerholt, and H. Andersson, "A multi-period analysis of the integrated item-sharing and crowdshipping problem," *European Journal of Operational Research*, vol. 292, no. 2, pp. 483–499, 2021.

[13] H. Shen and J. Lin, "Investigation of crowdshipping delivery trip production with real-world data," *Transportation Research Part E: Logistics and Transportation Review*, vol. 143, p. 102106, 2020.

[14] L. Kung and G. Zhong, "The optimal pricing strategy for two-sided platform delivery in the sharing economy," *Transportation Research Part E: Logistics and Transportation Review*, vol. 101, pp. 1–12, 2017.

[15] T. Le, S. Ukkusuri, J. Xue, and T. Van Woensel, "Designing pricing and compensation schemes by integrating matching and routing models for crowd-shipping systems," *Transportation Research Part E: Logistics and Transportation Review*, vol. 149, p. 102209, 2017.

[16] A. Ermagun and A. Stathopoulos, "To bid or not to bid: An empirical study of the supply determinants of crowd-shipping," *Transportation Research Part A: Policy and Practice*, vol. 116, pp. 468–483, 2018.

[17] N. Boysen, S. Emde, and S. Schwerdfeger, "Crowdshipping by employees of distribution centers: Optimization approaches for matching supply and demand," *European Journal of Operational Research*, vol. 296, no. 2, pp. 539–556, 2022.

[18] Y. Lan, F. Liu, W. Ng, M. Gui, and C. Lai, "Multi-objective two-echelon city dispatching problem with mobile satellites and crowd-shipping," *IEEE Transactions on Intelligent Transportation Systems*, vol. 23, no. 9, pp. 15 340–15 353, 2022.

[19] J. Fu, B. Moran, and P. G. Taylor, "A restless bandit model for resource allocation, competition and reservation," *Operations Research*, vol. 70, no. 1, pp. 416–431, 2022.

[20] M. Simoni and M. Winkenbach, "Crowdsourced on-demand food delivery: An order batching and assignment algorithm," *Transportation Research Part C: Emerging Technologies*, vol. 149, p. 104055, 2023.

[21] H. Akeb, B. Moncef, and B. Durand, "Building a collaborative solution in dense urban city settings to enhance parcel delivery: An effective crowd model in paris," *Transportation Research Part E: Logistics and Transportation Review*, vol. 119, pp. 223–233, 2018.

[22] J. Fu, L. Zhang, K. Huang, and Z. Liu, "A large-scale multi-rider matching problem with reneging passengers: Single source case," in *the 24th International Congress on Modelling and Simulation (MODSIM2021)*, Sydney, Australia, Dec. 2021, pp. 792–798.

[23] F. Torres, M. Gendreau, and W. Rei, "Vehicle routing with stochastic supply of crowd vehicles and time windows," *Transportation Science*, vol. 56, no. 3, pp. 631–653, 2022.

[24] H. Ghaderi, P. Tsai, L. Zhang, and A. Moayedikia, "An integrated crowdshipping framework for green last mile delivery," *Sustainable Cities and Society*, vol. 78, p. 103552, 2022.

[25] K. Mousavi, M. Bodur, and M. J. Roorda, "Stochastic last-mile delivery with crowd-shipping and mobile depots," *Transportation Science*, vol. 56, no. 3, pp. 612–630, 2022.

[26] K. Gdowska, A. Viana, and J. P. Pedroso, "Stochastic last-mile delivery with crowdshipping," *Transportation research procedia*, vol. 30, pp. 90–100, 2018.

[27] N. P. Farazi, B. Zou, and T. Tulabandhula, "Dynamic on-demand crowdshipping using constrained and heuristics-embedded double dueling deep q-network," *Transportation Research Part E: Logistics and Transportation Review*, vol. 166, p. 102890, 2022.

[28] J. Dötterl, R. Bruns, J. Dunkel, and S. Ossowski, "Evaluating crowdshipping systems with agent-based simulation," in *Multi-Agent Systems and Agreement Technologies*, N. Bassiliades, G. Chalkiadakis, and D. de Jonge, Eds. Cham: Springer International Publishing, 2020, pp. 396–411.

[29] G. Lee, W. Saad, and M. Bennis, "An online secretary framework for fog network formation with minimal latency," in *2017 IEEE International Conference on Communications (ICC)*, May 2017, pp. 1–6.

[30] The University of Melbourne, "Spartan," May 2023. [Online]. Available: https://dashboard.hpc.unimelb.edu.au/

[31] L. Dahle, H. Andersson, M. Christiansen, and M. Speranza, "The pickup and delivery problem with time windows and occasional drivers," *Computers and Operations Research*, vol. 109, pp. 122–133, 2019.

[32] C. Triki, "Using combinatorial auctions for the procurement of occasional drivers in the freight transportation: A case-study," *Journal of Cleaner Production*, vol. 304, p. 127057, 2021.

LookAhead - A New Approach for Event Handling in Co-Simulation by Predicting State Events

Felix Tischer
VIRTUAL VEHICLE Research Center
Inffeldgasse 21a, 8010 Graz, Austria
Email: Felix.Tischer@v2c2.at

Simon Genser
VIRTUAL VEHICLE Research Center
Inffeldgasse 21a, 8010 Graz, Austria
Email: Simon.Genser@v2c2.at

Daniel Watzenig
VIRTUAL VEHICLE Research Center
Inffeldgasse 21a, 8010 Graz, Austria
Email: Daniel.Watzenig@v2c2.at
Graz University of Technology
Institute of Automation and Control
Inffeldgasse 21/B/I, 8010 Graz, Austria
Email: daniel.watzenig@tugraz.at

Martin Benedikt
VIRTUAL VEHICLE Research Center
Inffeldgasse 21a, 8010 Graz, Austria
Email: Martin.Benedikt@v2c2.at
SETLabs Research GmbH
Elsenheimerstraße 55, 80687 Munich, Germany
Email: Martin.Benedikt@setlabs.de

***Abstract*— Hybrid systems consisting of discrete state events in otherwise continuous systems pose a significant challenge in co-simulation, as these events can lead to large errors depending on when they occur during a coupling time step. The coupling step size thus needed to correctly simulate state events can be significantly smaller than for the continuous part, resulting in an overall reduced coupling step size and longer and more expensive simulations. By dynamically adapting the coupling step size whenever an event is imminent, hybrid co-simulation can be improved significantly when compared to fixed-step co-simulation algorithms. This can be accomplished by predicting upcoming state events in advance. In an example simulation, this improves precision by a factor of 30 and decreases the number of coupling steps by a factor of 7.**

***Key words*—co-simulation, non-iterative co-simulation, hybrid simulation, event handling**

I. Introduction

In simulation, an event is defined as a system change that occurs instantly at a discrete point in time. The manner of change is not specified, and can include changes in state, models, or in the simulation behavior itself. A simulation that incorporates dynamic, continuous changes as well as discrete events is called a hybrid simulation [1] [2].

A physical system described by differential equations that is controlled by an electronic device, for example an autonomous vehicle or a smart power grid, is called a Cyber-Physical System (CPS), and is a prime example for hybrid simulations. The increasing importance of such systems makes it necessary to develop simulation tools that are able to handle them in a reliable and efficient manner [3].

An important tool in industrial development is co-simulation, where individual parts of a larger, complex system are being simulated simultaneously [4]. There, a master algorithm coordinates the simulation of the underlying subsystems by periodically exchanging information between them [5].

These subsystems are model components that contain their own solvers. They can thus have different solver step sizes, but are synchronized at regular intervals, the coupling time step, which is a property of the co-simulation and has a strong influence on the performance and accuracy of the co-simulation.

Events are especially challenging in co-simulation [6], as their time of occurrence is usually not known in advance, and if they occur in a subsystem between coupling time steps, they can introduce a large error in other subsystems as their correct state is only communicated at the next synchronization time.

By the condition of their occurrence, events can be classified as time events and state events. A time event occurs at specific points in time, and its occurrence is thus known in advance. A state event occurs when the model is in a certain state, like a variable reaching some threshold value. The time when a state event occurs is unknown in advance.

In co-simulation, events can also be distinguished by whether they belong to one or more than one subsystem. A private event is an event that happens in a single subsystem and influences the others only indirectly by the changes it introduced in its own subsystem. A shared event is one which belongs to two or more subsystems and affects both directly, like a binary collision. It thus has to occur in all participating subsystems at the same time [7].

The Functional Mock-up Interface (FMI) is an industry standard for co-simulation. The newest version, fmi3.0, added hybrid simulation capabilities for co-simulation FMUs (Functional Mock-up Units) in the form of clock variables whose "ticks" signal events [8]. The terminology and handling of events in this paper is based on the fmi3.0 specification [9].

The proposed algorithm attempts to improve hybrid co-simulation in a specific but common case: a system that is mostly defined by differential equations, but also contains discrete state events that happen rarely but have a large impact on model behaviour. This can be a frictional force changing sign, an autonomous vehicle performing an emergency braking, or as in the example here, collisions in a spring-damper-mass system.

To hit these events correctly, such systems often have to be co-simulated with a coupling step size that is far smaller than necessary with regards to the continuous behaviour. A lot of calculation time can be saved with an adaptive step size that is large by default, and smaller when a state event is imminent. By evaluating the current state of the system via event indicators, state events are predicted (even though their exact time is still unknown) sufficiently in advance, and the coupling time step is then reduced.

The next section describes how events are defined in the LookAhead algorithm. Section III then describes the algorithm, and Section IV showcases it with an example co-simulation. Section V then summarizes the work and discusses future developments.

II. Definition of Event Indicators

Define an event indicator as the complete set of functions which indicate an event:

$$Z = \{\, z_i(\vec{u}, \vec{y}, \vec{p}) \mid E \Leftrightarrow z_i \leq 0 \,\forall\, i\} \qquad (1)$$

The elements of this set are functions whose arguments are the inputs $\vec{u}$, the outputs $\vec{y}$, and the parameters $\vec{p}$ of the corresponding subsystem. Each function represents a condition for the event E that is met if the function evaluates to a value less than or equal to zero. Let these functions be called event conditions. Then, E occurring is equivalent to all z_i being less than or equal to zero. We can reformulate this condition as

$$E \Leftrightarrow \max_i z_i \leq 0 \qquad (2)$$

To ensure that an event happens only at a single time instant, the functions in Z have to be set up in a way such that at least one function returns a positive value after the event so that its conditions are no longer fulfilled afterwards. As the subsystem cannot control its inputs $\vec{u}$, this generally has to be accomplished by changing its outputs $\vec{u}$. The event can also change the parameters $\vec{p}$ or even the event indicator Z in case of models that support such functionalities.

The z_i are not directly dependent on time but its arguments are; we therefore denote $z_i(\vec{u}(t), \vec{y}(t), \vec{p}(t)) = z_i(t)$. As an event can lead to discontinuities in its arguments, $z_i(t)$ are not guaranteed to be continuous functions; but they are continuous on all intervals where no events occur.

Then, assuming that $z_i(t)$ are continuous right before an upcoming event, $\max_i z_i$ is also continuous, and we can replace (2) with a stricter condition:

$$E \Leftrightarrow \max_i z_i = 0 \qquad (3)$$

This means that the event happens as the last of its z_i crosses the x-axis. As the execution of an event changes at least one z_i to be positive afterwards, the event E only happens at these discrete points in time t_E. $\max_i z_i$ is thus always non-negative, and zero exactly at the event times t_E.

III. Description of LookAhead Algorithm

A co-simulation scenario with parallel scheduling is considered, where all subsystems calculate their coupling time steps in parallel and exchange their inputs and outputs afterwards.

This is done by the master algorithm, which orchestrates the co-simulation by signalling the subsystems to calculate time steps, and enables communication between them by requesting outputs and setting inputs. Each subsystem contains a model and, if necessary, handles translating these signals to the standard the contained model uses. The basic co-simulation loop then looks like this:

```
1: while t < t_stop − t_step do
2:    for all subsystem in system do
3:       subsystem.DoStep(t, t_step)
4:    end for
5:    for all connection in connections do
6:       connection.target.Set() ← connection.source.Get()
7:    end for
8:    t ← t + t_step
9: end while
```

Fig. 1. Basic co-simulation loop

In line 3, all subsystems in the co-simulation calculate one coupling time step. Later in line 6, the subsystems exchange data with each other according to their connections. Finally in line 8, the simulation time advances by the coupling step size before commencing to the next.

The LookAhead algorithm consists of two parts. One part is contained in a subsystem (Local LookAhead), while the other one is part of the master algorithm (Main LookAhead).

A. *Local LookAhead*

A subsystem containing state events can be equipped with a Local LookAhead routine (Algorithm 2) to predict its events and communicate them to the master algorithm. For each event, an event indicator set Z is included in the subsystem. The event conditions z in this set have to be provided manually (for now; see Section V for upcoming work on automatic event indicator construction). These z can only depend on locally accessible variables.

The local LookAhead algorithm then gets called at the end of each coupling time step to predict if an event will occur soon, and does so in a manner independent of the number of event indicators or the sizes of the event indicator sets.

1: **for** Z in list of event indicators **do**
2: $t_0 \leftarrow -1$
3: **for** z in Z **do**
4: $z_{prev} \leftarrow z_{now}$
5: $z_{now} \leftarrow z(t)$
6: $z_{next} \leftarrow z_{now} + d * (z_{now} - z_{prev})$
7: **if** $z_{next} < 0$ **then**
8: **if** $z_{now} > 0$ **then**
9: $t_{0,new} \leftarrow c * \Delta t * z_{now}/(z_{prev} - z_{now})$
10: **if** $t_{0,new} < t_{min}$ **then**
11: $t_{0,new} \leftarrow t_{min}$
12: **end if**
13: **else**
14: $t_{0,new} \leftarrow -1$
15: **end if**
16: $t_0 \leftarrow \max(t_0, t_{0,new})$
17: **else**
18: $t_0 \leftarrow -1$
19: break
20: **end if**
21: **end for**
22: **if** $t_0 \geq t_{min}$ **then**
23: append t_0 to t_E
24: **end if**
25: **end for**
26: **if** t_E not empty **then**
27: **return** $\min t_E$
28: **else**
29: **return** -1
30: **end if**

Fig. 2. Local LookAhead algorithm

For each event indicator, the local LookAhead algorithm takes the current and previous values of the event indicators z (z_{now} and z_{prev}, respectively) to extrapolate the value z_{next} that it will have d (the forecasting factor, $d > 1$) time steps in the future in line 6. For this, the algorithm requires the current coupling step size Δt (which can be smaller than the default value if the previous time step was already shortened by LookAhead) as an input from the master algorithm.

If all z_{next} are below zero, the event is predicted to happen. On the other hand, if one $z_{next} > 0$ (line 17) the event is not predicted to happen, and the algorithm continues on to the next event indicator. If an event indicator is predicted to be negative in the future but is positive at the current time, the time until zero-crossing t_0 gets interpolated in line 9. To prevent overestimation, a safety factor $c \in (0, 1]$ is introduced that reduces t_0.

In case that t_0 is less than the minimal solver step size t_{min}, $t_0 \leftarrow t_{min}$ (line 11). If z_{now} is already negative, t_0 is set to -1 (line 18) as it is not relevant to event time estimation. If all z_{next} are negative, the corresponding event is predicted to happen at the time when the last zero-crossing happens. The event time for the predicted event is then the maximum value of all t_0, as this is the time where (3) is fulfilled, which is then appended to the list of predicted events t_E in line 23.

After iterating through all events of the subsystem, the minimum of all t_E will be returned (line 27). If no event is predicted to happen, LookAhead will return -1 in line 29 to signal that its return value has to be ignored.

B. Main LookAhead

As shown in Algorithm 1, the master algorithm advances its own time by the same constant time step after each iteration of calculating and exchanging outputs. The main LookAhead extends Algorithm 1 to make it possible to adapt this time step.

while $t < t_{stop} - t_{step,max}$ **do**
for all subsystem in system **do**
subsystem.DoStep(t, t_{step})
end for
for all connection in connections **do**
connection.target.Set() $\leftarrow$ connection.source.Get()
end for
$t \leftarrow t + t_{step}$
list $t_{next} \leftarrow \{t_{step,max}\}$
for all subsystem in system **do**
if subsystem.supportsLookAhead **then**
$t_E \leftarrow$ subsystem.lookAhead(t_{step})
if $t_E > 0$ **then**
append t_E to t_{next}
end if
end if
$t_{step} \leftarrow \min t_{next}$
end for
end while

Fig. 3. Co-simulation loop containing main LookAhead

After completing the conventional co-simulation loop, the master algorithm calls the LookAhead function in every subsystem that supports it. Each returns either -1 if no event is predicted to happen, or returns the predicted time until the next event t_E, in which case this time gets appended to a list of event times t_{next}. The master algorithm then chooses the smallest element of that list as its next time step. If no subsystem returns an event time or if event times are larger than the default time step, this default time step $t_{step,max}$ gets selected.

IV. Example on a Spring-Damper-Mass System

The example is taken from [7] with minimal adaptations.

Two masses are vertically connected in a spring-damper system; the upper mass m_1 is connected to the ceiling with a spring of stiffness k_1 and dampening d_1, and m_1 and the lower mass m_2 are connected together via a second spring of stiffness k_2 and d_2. Each mass has a position x_i and a velocity v_i. The masses are realized as blocks with vertical size $2\Delta x$. Figure 4 illustrates this system.

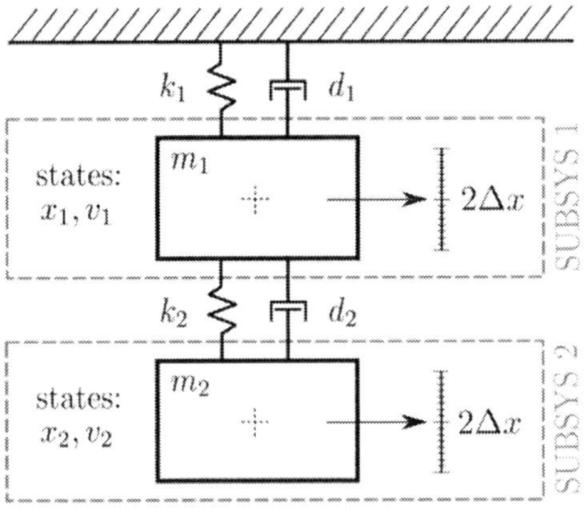

Fig. 4. Setup of the spring-damper-mass system. The figure and example have been taken from [7], with the slight adaptation of changing Δx to $2\Delta x$.

The upper mass can collide with the ceiling and the two masses can collide with each other. These collisions can be realised as state events; they are an instantaneously occurring change triggered by the system being in a certain state.

This system is a good example to demonstrate LookAhead as it is a continuous system that encounters multiple events when the initial conditions are set up correctly, and whose trajectory can diverge greatly between the monolithic simulation and the co-simulation when these events are not handled well enough in the co-simulation.

A. Co-simulation Setup

For co-simulation, the system is split up into upper and lower mass. Each one of the masses takes the other one's position and speed as inputs $\vec{u}$, and provides its own position and speed as outputs $\vec{y}$.

$$\begin{aligned} \dot{y}_1 &= y_2 \\ \dot{y}_2 &= -\frac{k_1+k_2}{m_1}y_1 - \frac{d_1+d_2}{m_1}y_2 + \frac{k_2}{m_1}u_1 + \frac{d_2}{m_1}u_2 - g \end{aligned} \tag{4}$$

Let event 1 be the collision of the upper mass with the ceiling. Mass 1 then gets reflected downwards (6) when it touches the ceiling and has positive speed (5). Let event 2 be the collision of the two masses. Their reflected velocities depend on the masses (8). Similar to event 1, event 2 occurs when the masses touch and move towards each other (7).

$$Z_1 = \{z_1 = -(y_1 + \Delta x), z_2 = -y_2\} \tag{5}$$

$$E_1 : y_2' = -y_2 \Leftrightarrow \max_{z \in Z_1} z = 0 \tag{6}$$

$$Z_2 = \{z_1 = y_1 - u_1 - 2\Delta x, z_2 = y_2 - u_2\} \tag{7}$$

$$E_2 : y_2' = \frac{m_1 - m_2}{m_1 + m_2}y_2 + \frac{2m_2}{m_1 + m_2}u_2 \Leftrightarrow \max_{z \in Z_2} z = 0 \tag{8}$$

Subsystem 1 simulates the trajectory of the upper mass, and contains its equations of motions (4) as well as both events.

$$\begin{aligned} \dot{y}_1 &= y_2 \\ \dot{y}_2 &= -\frac{k_1+k_2}{m_2}y_1 - \frac{d_1+d_2}{m_2}y_2 + \frac{k_2}{m_2}u_1 + \frac{d_2}{m_2}u_2 - g, \end{aligned} \tag{9}$$

$$Z = \{z_1 = u_1 - y_1 - 2\Delta x, z_2 = u_2 - y_2\}$$

$$E_2 : y_2' = \frac{m_2 - m_1}{m_1 + m_2}y_2 + \frac{2m_1}{m_1 + m_2}u_2 \Leftrightarrow \max_{z \in Z} z = 0 \tag{10}$$

Subsystem 2 simulates the lower mass, and contains its equations of motions (9) and event 2 (10).

Event 1 is a private state event. As it occurs in two subsystems at the same time, event 2 is a shared state event. The relative velocity between objects changes sign after a collision, thus both events no longer fulfill their second conditions after the event.

For the monolithic solution, the equations of motions are solved as a single system of four equations, and the events are implemented by checking the event conditions after each solver step.

Regarding the setup of the LookAhead routine, the safety and forecasting factors have to be chosen. The value of the safety factor $c = 0.9$ has been chosen based on the behaviour of the variables relevant for event prediction. On the co-simulation step time scale, the positions and velocities of the two masses behave quite linear, meaning that the extrapolation of z inside the LookAhead algorithm only has a small error compared to the real values. Thus, c can be chosen with a high value near 1. If the event conditions z were less predictable, the safety factor would need to be smaller in order to prevent the algorithm from missing events.

The forecasting factor of $d \leq 2$ is chosen similarly.

B. Simulation Results

In the upper part of Figure 5, the trajectories of three simulations are compared. The solid blue lines are the trajectories of the co-simulation where both subsystems contain a local LookAhead instance. The green dashed lines are the trajectory of a co-simulation without LookAhead capability, and the red dotted lines are the monolithic solution as a reference. The upper mass collides with the ceiling when its position is $x_1 = -\Delta x$, indicated by the horizontal line. The lower part of Figure 5 shows the absolute error

$$e_{pos} := |x_1 - \hat{x}_1| + |x_2 - \hat{x}_2|$$

for both co-simulations, where $\hat{x}_i$ are the positions of the reference solution. It is easy to see how LookAhead improves the performance of the co-simulation. The root mean square of this error,

$$e_{pos,rms} := \sqrt{\frac{1}{n}\sum_{i=0}^{n}(|x_{1,n} - \hat{x}_{1,n}| + |x_{1,n} - \hat{x}_{1,n}|)^2},$$

is $e_{rms} = \mathbf{0.12}$ and $e_{rms} = \mathbf{3.65}$, with and without LookAhead respectively. The default time step of the co-simulation was $t_{step} = 0.08s$, calculating to $t_{stop} = 20s$ in

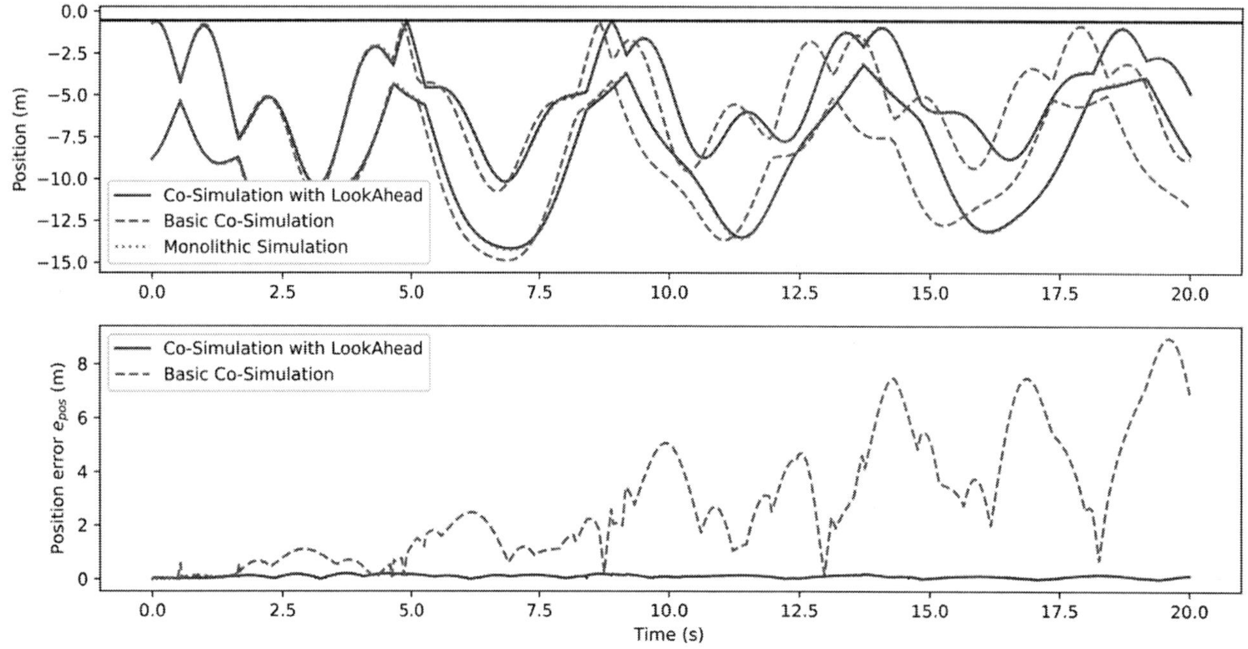

Fig. 5. Comparison of trajectories of the two masses. Top: total positions of the two masses in each simulation case. Bottom: Position error with respect to the monolithic simulation result.

250 steps. LookAhead introduced only 32 additional steps. This means that, with the same base coupling step size, the error improves by $\mathbf{96.7\%}$ or a factor of $\mathbf{30.3}$ while only taking 12.8%. more steps.

To achieve an error equal or less than that without LookAhead, $t_{step} = 0.01$ is required, taking 2000 steps instead with an error of $e_{rms} = 0.07$, meaning that, for a desired error limit, LookAhead reduces the number of steps by $\mathbf{85.9\%}$ or a factor of $\mathbf{7.1}$.

Figure 6 shows two detail views of the monolithic and LookAhead simulations. Approaching the event in the top image, coupling step size gets increasingly smaller until the event occurs, after which the step size returns to default. In the bottom half no event occurs, but as their extrapolated trajectories intermittently cross each other, LookAhead decreases step size for a few steps before returning to default once it is clear no event will happen.

V. Summary, Conclusion and Future Work

A. Summary

By defining functions that indicate the occurrence of state events, it is possible to estimate imminent state events a few time steps prior to their occurrence by interpolating these event condition functions. Then, the coupling time step can be adapted to hit these event times more precise.

Compared to a constant time step simulation, where events can happen at random points between time steps, this can significantly improve the error, especially in chaotic systems like the one shown in the example.

B. Conclusion

The proposed LookAhead algorithm vastly improves the performance of hybrid systems where only a small number of events occur during co-simulation, while keeping calculation time low. The coupling step size is only reduced when necessary, and the additional overhead for event prediction is kept as small as possible. In this manner, the error was reduced by a factor of 30 with the same step size. To achieve the same error without implementing LookAhead in the master algorithm, the co-simulation takes 7 times more steps.

This is much more efficient than choosing a smaller coupling step size in general or taking an iterative approach [10], as many models do not support this. If they do, saving and (re)setting states is computationally expensive as well, especially with growing complexity of the models or the co-simulation, while LookAhead's complexity only depends on the number of events.

C. Future Work

Future work is mostly focused on usability. In the example, the event indicators have to be set up manually and are independent of their actual implementation in the subsystems, as these are treated as black-boxes. It would be favourable if this step could be automated in cases where many events are present or it is not known how they depend on the inputs.

Also, there exist other scheduling paradigms besides parallel execution. Thus, for general coupling schemes the main LookAhead algorithm has to be adapted, depending on how and when signal exchange takes place.

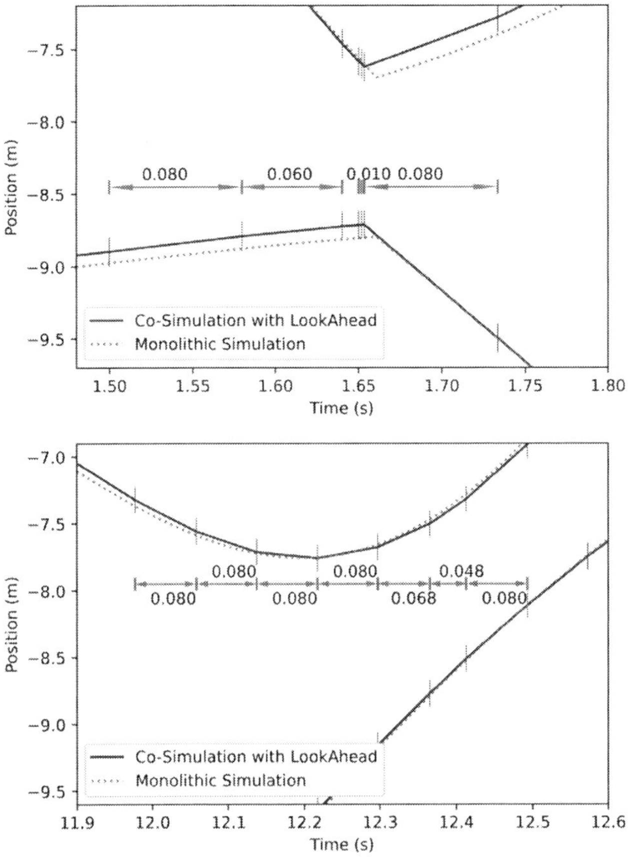

Fig. 6. Detailed views of LookAhead predicting events. The vertical lines mark the synchronization time points in the co-simulation. The lines get denser as they approach an event, and return to the default communication step size afterwards. Top: A shared event. Bottom: Prediction of an event that does not happen.

This could be combined with an example of an industrial application, where the performance of the LookAhead algorithm can be compared with different coupling methods, iterative co-simulation, and other methods for improving co-simulation results.

Finally, LookAhead is planned to be implemented in the ICOS co-simulation tool developed at Virtual Vehicle Research GmbH, that is contained in the Model.CONNECT™ co-simulation platform developed by AVL List GmbH [11].

ACKNOWLEDGMENT

The publication was written at Virtual Vehicle Research GmbH in Graz, Austria. The authors would like to acknowledge the financial support within the COMET K2 Competence Centers for Excellent Technologies from the Austrian Federal Ministry for Climate Action (BMK), the Austrian Federal Ministry for Labour and Economy (BMAW), the Province of Styria (Dept. 12) and the Styrian Business Promotion Agency (SFG). The Austrian Research Promotion Agency (FFG) has been authorised for the programme management.

REFERENCES

[1] N. Mustafee, J. Powell, S. Brailsford, S. Diallo, J. Padilla, and A. Tolk, "Hybrid simulation studies and hybrid simulation systems: Definitions, challenges, and benefits," in *2015 Winter Simulation Conference (WSC)*, 12 2015.

[2] A. Pinto, A. Sangiovanni-Vincentelli, L. P. Carloni, and R. Passerone, "Interchange formats for hybrid systems: Review and proposal," vol. 3414, pp. 526–541, Springer Verlag, 2005.

[3] G. Schweiger, G. Engel, J.-P. Schöggl, I. Hafner, T. S. Nouidui, and C. Gomes, "Co-simulation - an empirical survey: Applications, recent developments and future challenges," *SNE Simulation Notes Europe*, vol. 30, pp. 73–76, 6 2020.

[4] C. Gomes, C. Thule, D. Broman, P. G. Larsen, and H. Vangheluwe, "Co-simulation: A survey," *ACM Computing Surveys*, vol. 51, 4 2018.

[5] R. Kübler and W. Schiehlen, "Two methods of simulator coupling," *Mathematical and Computer Modelling of Dynamical Systems*, vol. 6, pp. 113 – 93, 2000.

[6] F. Cremona, M. Lohstroh, D. Broman, E. A. Lee, M. Masin, and S. Tripakis, "Hybrid co-simulation: it's about time," *Software and Systems Modeling*, vol. 18, pp. 1655–1679, 6 2019.

[7] D. Dejaco and M. Benedikt, "A novel approach for handling discontinuities in non-iterative co-simulation," in *Proceedings of the 7th International Conference on Simulation and Modeling Methodologies, Technologies and Applications*, SIMULTECH 2017, (Setubal, PRT), p. 288–295, SCITEPRESS - Science and Technology Publications, Lda, 2017.

[8] D. Broman, L. Greenberg, E. A. Lee, M. Masin, S. Tripakis, and M. Wetter, "Requirements for hybrid cosimulation standards," in *Proceedings of the 18th International Conference on Hybrid Systems: Computation and Control*, HSCC '15, (New York, NY, USA), p. 179–188, Association for Computing Machinery, 2015.

[9] C. Gomes, T. Blochwitz, C. Bertsch, K. Wernersson, K. Schuch, P. R., O. Kotte, I. Zacharias, M. Blesken, T. Sommer, M. Najafi, and A. Junghanns, "The fmi 3.0 standard interface for clocked and scheduled simulations," *Proceedings of 14th Modelica Conference 2021, Linköping, Sweden, September 20-24, 2021*, vol. 181, pp. 27–36, 9 2021.

[10] F. Cremona, M. Lohstroh, D. Broman, M. D. Natale, E. A. Lee, and S. Tripakis, "Step revision in hybrid co-simulation with fmi," pp. 173–183, Institute of Electrical and Electronics Engineers Inc., 12 2016.

[11] AVL, "Model.connect™, co-simulation tool for the coupled simulation of multiple models and different tools as well as the integration with real-time systems.." https://www.avl.com/en/simulation-solutions/software-offering/simulation-tools-z/modelconnect. Accessed: 2023-08-24.

A Supply Chain Disruption Framework for Discrete Event Simulation

Andrew Greasley
Dept. of Engineering Systems & Supply Chain Management
Aston University
Birmingham, UK
e-mail: a.greasley@aston.ac.uk

Daniel Chicksand
Dept. of Management
University of Birmingham
Birmingham, UK
e-mail: d.chicksand@bham.ac.uk

Abstract—**This article presents a supply chain disruption framework for discrete event simulation based on the analysis of the prior literature. The aim is to develop a better understanding of the elements that are required to meet the challenge of using discrete event simulation in this application. The framework identifies the main elements in terms of the disruption event, supply chain configuration, supply chain resilience and supply chain performance metrics. The review also identifies challenges for the use of discrete-event simulation in this way including the representation of rare disruption events and time-series interpretation of disruption events.**

Keywords-supply chain disruption, discrete event simulation.

I. INTRODUCTION

Discrete Event Simulation (DES) is usually considered a stand-alone software tool that is used to assess the steady-state performance of manufacturing and service processes. However recently it has been used to undertake the analysis of the effect of transient disruptive events in a variety of supply chain settings such as food retail [1], LED panel light manufacturing [2], medicine supply [3] and forestry log export [4]. In this context the lack of empirical data that could be used to understand these events is to some extent overcome by the use of structured experimentation using computer simulation experiments [5].

The purpose of this article is to review existing work on the use of DES to analyse disruptive events in a supply chain context. From this review a framework has been developed that identifies the key attributes of the combination of disruptive events, the supply chain configuration and supply chain resilience factors that lead to supply chain performance. By identifying key attributes associated with supply chain disruptions, this framework will provide a basis on which to develop a DES model of disruption events and measure their effect on supply chain performance.

II. REVIEW OF THE USE OF DES TO ANALYSE DISRUPTIVE EVENTS IN THE SUPPLY CHAIN

The review examines supply chain disruption in terms of the nature of the disruption event itself, the supply chain configuration, the supply chain features and relationships that lead to a level of supply chain resilience and supply chain performance metrics used to assess the response to disruption events.

A. *Disruption Event*

A disruption can be defined as an unplanned and unanticipated event that disrupts the normal flow of goods and materials in the supply chain [6]. An event that has the potential to occur, but has not yet done so, can be referred to in terms of 'risk' [7]. As well as the direct impact of a disruption on the supply chain we may need to consider the ripple effect defined as a disruption in a supply chain node that can spread to neighbouring nodes or links [8]. The ripple effect is associated with low-frequency, high-impact disturbance risks [8].

In the context of a supply chain for the source of risk (that leads to a disruption event) [9] define two main categories of internal risk and supply chain risk.

- Internal risks can be categorised as the internal risk of the process (value-adding processes) and the internal risk of control (systems which govern how a firm controls the processes).
- Supply Chain risks can be categorised as external to the firm but internal to the supply chain network (either downstream demand or upstream supply risks) or external to the supply chain network (events in the environment such as natural disasters or socio-political events).

Manners-Bell [10] states that although supply chain risks are the most relevance in the supply chain context, internal risks of process and control can also impact the wider supply chain.

In terms of DES models of the source of risks leading to disruption events, [11] models a combination of the following:

- internal firm risks such as machine breakdowns and internal quality problems
- internal supply chain risks such as delays in contracting with suppliers and raw material shortage
- external supply chain risks such as earthquakes and computer Denial of Service events

Borgos and Ivanov [1] model disruption events related to the external supply chain risk of the COVID-19 pandemic in terms of internal supply chain risks leading to shutdowns at supplier's factories, bottlenecks in transportation and panic buying by customers.

In terms characterising a disruption event, [5] provide the following generic attributes:

- length (number of time periods over which the shock manifests itself),
- magnitude (the size of the initial negative impact, and the extent to which the shock subsequently reduces supply chain performance over time,
- shape (the way in which the disruption manifests itself – a step function, a ramp etc.)
- number (number and frequency of disruption that occur during a given event).

B. Supply Chain Configuration

In terms of the supply chain configuration, this can be described by the use of a supply chain map such as in [2]. Christopher [12] emphasises the importance of managing the critical nodes and links in the supply chain. MacCarthy et al. [13] define the minimum information for a supply chain map as nodes, the participants of the supply chain and links, how the participants are connected. Primary participants contribute direct to value-adding activities in the supply chain process, but we may also need to incorporate secondary participants such as third-party logistics providers in our analysis. The primary flows modelled by DES in the review are material flows, such as in [14] but information and financial flows could also be modelled.

C. Supply Chain Resilience Factors

In terms of factors that impact the resilience of the supply chain to disruption events, [15] distinguishes between the physical features of a supply chain such as its design matched to demand, shape, stocks, capacity, agility/flexibility and supply chain relationships such as collaboration and visibility. In addition [5] model the connectivity relationship between supply chain actors.

In terms of supply chain physical features examples cover the use of higher stocks and spare capacity, such as Garrido Rios [11] who provides an analysis of on-hand inventory and short-term manufacturing capacity. Ivanov [14] studies the use of a policy of backup capacity - using capacity in owned plants in the region and using the capacity of owned plants in neighbouring countries. In terms of supply chain relationships, [16] study the use of the policy of alternative suppliers and [2] study the use of backup suppliers.

D. Supply Chain Performance

In terms of measuring supply chain performance when submitted to disruption events, [17] define performance measures of speed of recovery, financial cost and customer impact. Borgos and Ivanov [1] define performance measures of profit, revenue, costs, delivery time, inventory levels, order backlog (orders lacking products) and late orders.

As well as direct supply chain design and operations measures most studies aim to provide a measure of supply chain resilience which is defined by [18] as requiring two capacities of resistance (ability to delay a disruption and reduce the impact once the disruption occurs) and recovery (ability to recover from a disruption). Garrido Rios [11] defines (static) resilience as a function of fill rate which is defined as the number of backorders and lost orders as a proportion of total orders. Borgos and Ivanov [1] use the service level ratio of on-time orders to overall number of outgoing orders as an indicator of disruption and recovery. Moosavi et al. [2] use the resilience metric from [19] and [5] provides an overall measure of resilience (defined as the relative percentage of functionality over time) derived from the three measures of the number of time periods in which a negative change in inventory is observed, the total negative change in inventory over the course of these time periods and the average negative change in inventory over this same interval.

III. DEPLOYING THE FRAMEWORK FOR DES

Based on the review a framework is presented which can be used when using DES to analyse disruptive events that impact on the supply chain (Fig. 1). Disruption events act on the configuration of supply chain design and combine with supply chain resilience factors to produce a level of supply chain performance. The supply chain resilience factors will be aspects of the current supply chain design that have an effect on supply chain performance. They can also be part of the simulation experimental design to analyse the effect of disruption events on future supply chain configurations.

We can now proceed to investigate how to operationalise the elements in the framework to enable its representation as a DES model.

Macdonald et al., [5] model the characteristic of a generic disruption event directly. If we wish to model a disruption event that has been derived from a source of risk, we will need to operationalise this event by characteristics of its length, magnitude, shape and number. For example, Garrido Rios [11] operationalises disruption events deriving from risks such as machine breakdown, using probability distributions for the number of occurrences and length of disruption. Uniform distributions are used to represent the time between disruption events based on the assumption that the likelihood of the event remains constant over the simulated time period.

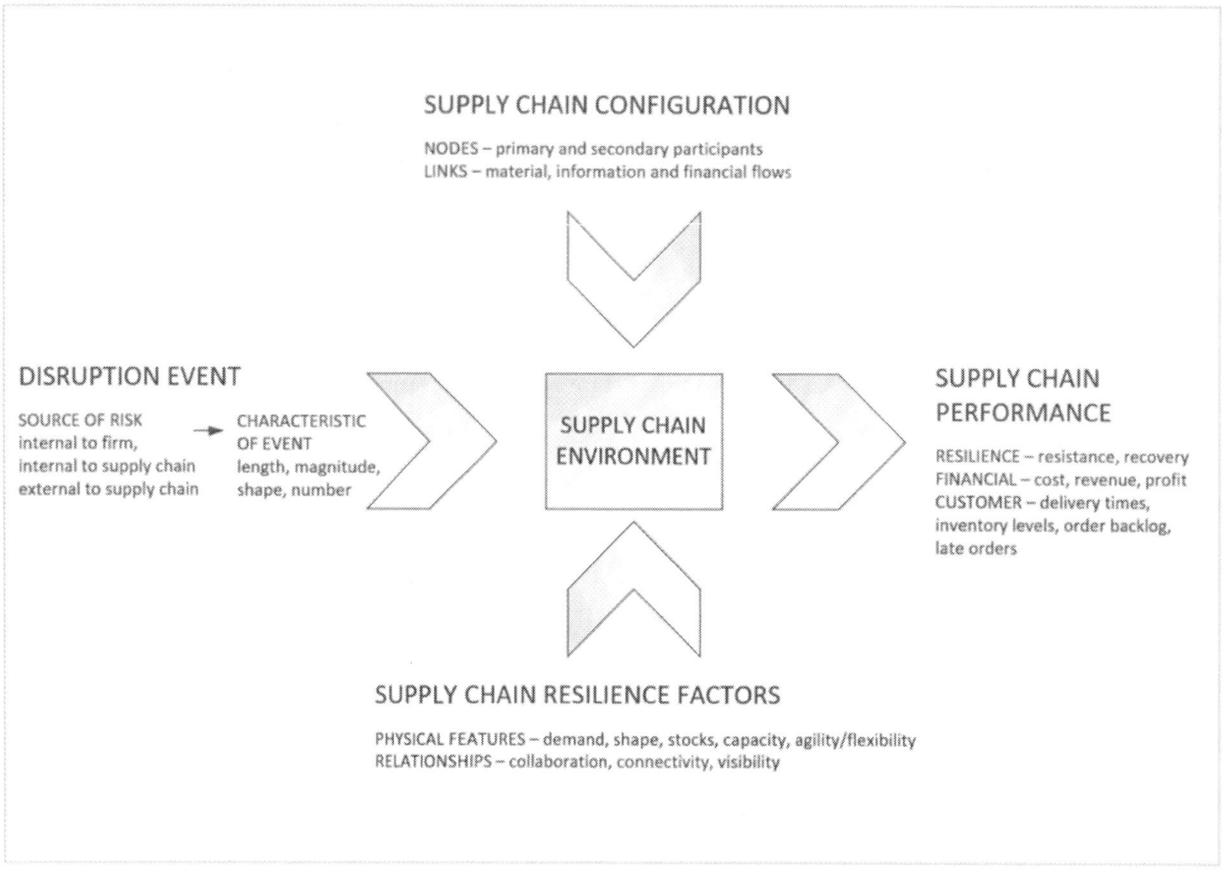

Figure 1. Supply Chain Disruption Framework for Discrete Event Simulation

In terms of supply chain configuration, the conceptual modelling stage of the DES study will require us to develop a diagrammatic representation, usually in the form of a process map, of the explanatory model [20]. MacCarthy et al. [13] argue that the degree of mapping the supply chain depends on the purpose and so introduce a classification of supply chain maps based on a hierarchy of supply systems. This may require high level supply chain and supply network maps to be decomposed to the process map level (as presented in a hierarchy for supply systems mapping, [13]) to enable modelling of material flows by the DES. To define the supply chain configuration in a DES, [21] organise the process map around the Supply Chain Operations Reference (SCOR) model categories of Source, Make and Deliver.

In terms of supply chain resilience factors, the current resilience of the supply chain can be assessed for a range of disruption events. In addition, the use of simulation scenarios incorporating either physical or relationship design changes can be employed. For example, connectivity is operationalised for a DES study by [5] by expressing connectivity between supply chain partners as a value between 0 (no connectivity) to 1 (full connectivity). Full connectivity means that the full effect of the disruption event would be passed between supply chain partners.

Finally supply chain performance can be expressed using traditional DES measures such as financial and customer-oriented metrics. These can be reported by simulating over multiple replications to provide confidence intervals around average performance across these metrics [20]. In terms of the concept of resilience this metric will require operationalising, for example as inventory fill rate [11]. Resilience may also require a time-based analysis to identify the nature of the recovery from the disruption event in terms of its magnitude and length. Melnyk et al. [16] outline a procedure for dealing with time series data that uses a differencing technique combined with an outlier detection approach [22]. The outcome is the quantification of system performance in terms of measures that define resistance and recovery.

IV. SUMMARY

The framework identifies the elements that need to be incorporated into the DES model and provides a roadmap for determining suitable methods for operationalising these elements in the DES. However, further work is needed to meet the challenge of modelling supply chain disruption using DES. For example, the representation of rare disruption events, the impact of the ripple effect, supply chain mapping decomposition at the conceptual modelling stage and time-series interpretation of disruption events at the experimentation stage.

REFERENCES

[1] D. Borgos and D. Ivanov, "Food retail supply chain resilience and the COVID-19 pandemic: A digital twin-based impact analysis and improvement directions", Transportation Research Part E, vol. 152, 102412, 2021.

[2] J. Moosavi and S. Hosseini, "Simulation-based assessment of supply chain resilience with consideration of recovery strategies in the COVID-19 pandemic context", Computers and Industrial Engineering, vol. 160, 107593, 2021.

[3] J. Viana, K. van Oorschot and C. Ardal, "Assessing resilience of medicine supply chain networks to disruptions: a proposed hybrid simulation modelling framework", Proceedings of the 2021 Winter Simulation Conference, IEEE, 2021.

[4] P. Childerhouse, M. Al Aqqad, Q. Zhou, and C. Bezuidenhout, "Network resilience modelling: a New Zealand forestry supply chain case", The International Journal of Logistics Management, vol. 31, no. 2, pp. 291-311, 2020.

[5] J.R. Macdonald, C.W. Zobel, S.A. Melynk and S.E. Griffis, "Supply chain risk and resilience: theory building through structured experiments and simulation", International Journal of Production Research, vol. 56, no. 12, pp. 4337-4355, 2018.

[6] C.W. Craighead, J. Blackhurst, M.J. Rungtusanatham and R.B. Handfield, "The Severity of Supply Chain Disruptions: Design Characteristics and Mitigation Capabilities", Decision Sciences, vol. 38 no. 1, pp. 131-156, 2007.

[7] I. Manuj, J.T. Mentzer and M.R. Bowers, "Global Supply Chain Risk Management", Journal of Business Logistics, vol. 29, no. 1, 133-155, 2008

[8] A. Llaguno, J. Mula and F. Campuzano-Bolarin, "State of the art, conceptual framework and simulation analysis of the ripple effect on supply chains", International Journal of Production Research, vol. 60, no. 6, pp. 2044-2066, 2022.

[9] R. Mason-Jones and D. Towill, "Shrinking the supply chain uncertainty cycle", Control, September, pp. 17-22, 1998.

[10] J. Manners-Bell, "Supply Chain Risk Management: How to design and manage resilient supply chains", 3rd Edition, Kogan Page: London, 2020.

[11] D.A. Garrido Rios, "A Mixed-Method Study on the Effectiveness of a Buffering Strategy in the Relationship between Risks and Resilience", PhD Thesis. http://wrap.warwick.ac.uk/106605, 2017.

[12] M. Christopher, "Logistics and Supply Chain Management", Fifth Edition, FT Publishing: Harlow, 2016.

[13] B.L. MacCarthy, W.A.A. Ahmed and G. Demirel, "Mapping the supply chain: Why, what and how?", International Journal of Production Economics, vol. 250, 108688, 2022.

[14] D. Ivanov, "Disruption tails and revival policies: A simulation analysis of supply chain design and production-ordering systems in the recovery and post-disruption periods", Computers and Industrial Engineering, vol. 127, pp. 558-570, 2019.

[15] D. Waters, "Supply Chain Risk Management: Vulnerability and Resilience in Logistics", 2nd Edition, Kogan Page: London, 2011.

[16] S.A. Melnyk, C.W. Zobel, J.R. MacDonald and S.E. Griffis, "Making sense of transient responses in simulation studies", International Journal of Production Research, vol. 52, no. 3, pp. 617-632, 2014.

[17] J.R. Macdonald and T.M. Corsi, "Supply Chain Disruption Management: Severe Events, Recovery, and Performance", Journal of Business Logistics, vol. 34, no. 4, pp. 270-288, 2013.

[18] S.A. Melnyk, D.J. Closs, S.E. Griffis, C.W. Zobel and J.R. MacDonald, "Understanding supply chain resilience", Supply Chain Management Review, January/February, 2014.

[19] S.A. Torabi, M. Baghersad and S.A. Mansouri, "Resilient supplier selection and order allocation under operational and disruption risks", Transportation Research Part E, vol. 79, pp. 22-48, 2015.

[20] A. Greasley, "Simulation Modelling: Concepts, Tools and Practical Business Applications", Routledge:Abingdon, 2023.

[21] H. Carvalho, A.P. Barroso, V.H. Machedo, S. Azevedo and V. Cruz-Machado, "Supply chain redesign for resilience using simulation", Computers and Industrial Engineering, Vol. 62, pp. 329-341, 2012.

[22] L.M. Liu, "Time Series Analysis and Forecasting", Second Edition, Scientific Computing Associates Corp: Chicago, 2009.

How Marketing and Sales can Push and Accelerate Residential Refurbishment

Results of an Agent-based Simulation on pushing and accelerating Refurbishment Decisions

Mart Verhoog
Marketing and Communication Department
IU International University of Applied Sciences
Bad Honnef, Germany
e-mail: mart.verhoog@iu.org

Abstract—**Agent-based models can be used to assess the impact of different mixes of marketing and sales measures on homeowner's energetic refurbishment decision-making. During the last two decades, governments have been using especially marketing-like measures (e.g., mass media campaigns) to push residential refurbishment – for a large part unsuccessfully. Only recently, more sales-like activities (e.g., visits of energy consultants) have been offered for that purpose. The question now arises whether this will be a more successful approach. This paper addresses the research question asking what mix of marketing and sales measures is optimal to support homeowners during their refurbishment decision-making.**

Keywords— Agent-Based Modeling (ABM); refurbishment Decision-Making (DM); marketing and sales; empirically grounded.

I. Introduction and Motivation

Much research has been published about the importance of residential refurbishment for sustainability. Germany's building stock has been erected for the largest part before the existence of any energetic building standards. Furthermore, German homeowners tend to energetically refurbish their property slowly and doubtingly. Consequently, heating residential buildings consumes too much energy and is accompanied by a huge ecological footprint [1].

More recently, the dependence of many European countries on Russian gas for heating buildings and the war Russia has been fighting against Ukraine has recharged the debate that energy efficiency in housing should be improved and refurbishment should be speeded up to lessen the dependency on Russian gas.

This paper draws on a previous idea contribution of the author as discussed in [2]. It deals with the question asking how governments can optimally push homeowners in the direction of a positive refurbishing decision with the help of marketing and sales measures. In the past, governments used mass media campaigns to do this. More recently, local governments have been offering visits of energy consultants at a reduced (or even at no) charge to convince homeowners to refurbish. The question is whether there are optimal (cost efficient and concerning speed) mixes of marketing and sales measures that help homeowners make this decision positively. An empirically grounded Agent-Based Model for refurbishment is developed and the impact of different mixes of marketing and sales on refurbishment Decision-Making (DM) is simulated.

Science has applied ABM in the context of the current energy transition numerous times before. Du et al. [3] conclude in their review that ABM has been developed to model socio-demographic factors, housing factors, social influences, and environmental attitudes as drivers of DM in a context of energy transition. Most ABM, however, have focused on solar energy diffusion and less research was done to study refurbishment. Furthermore, Du et al. [3] conclude "Future studies can also evaluate the effectiveness of market-based policies [...]" (p. 8).

Jager already stated in 2007 that the effectiveness of marketing could benefit from social simulations like ABM [4]. He proposed different formalizations of the 4 P's commonly used in marketing to be implemented in ABM (Product, Price, Place and Promotion). Delre et al. [5] focus especially on promotional activities, which is the category where mass and personal communication can be classified. Until today, however, ABM applied in consumer behavior DM studies do not differentiate between marketing and sales.

For both the literature concerning DM in an energy transition context, and ABM literature in the field of marketing, modeling an optimal usage of marketing and sales to push residential refurbishment is an interesting contribution.

This paper is structured as follows. Section II briefly explains the key concepts used in this paper. Here, the Hierarchy Of Effects (HOE) model, the German Sinus lifestyle typology, and the ABM approach are discussed, as they are used to simulate the refurbishment DM of 17 Mi. homeowners in Germany. Section III discusses all specifics and details of the developed ABM for refurbishment. Finally, Section IV presents and discusses the modeling results and answers the research question of this paper.

II. Key Concepts used in this paper

The objective of commercial communication (or "touchpoints") is to have an impact on consumers and to support consumers in buying DM. A large body of research exists to assess this impact. HOE models represent a family of models that examine this impact of touchpoints on different steps in the buying behavior. In this logic, HOE models assume forthcoming steps in the DM process can only be reached when previous ones have been effectively completed. Consequently, the number of people who reach the next step in the process is usually reduced, compared to the previous step. This transfer from a previous step onto the next is called conversion. HOE models enable the calculation of transfer rates under the influence of communication – and as well under the influence of different kinds of communication: mass and personal communication.

Section I mentioned that ABM has not distinguished between marketing and sales until today. HOE models can do exactly this: The first stages in the model are primarily impacted by marketing (mass communication touchpoints), and the last stages primarily by sales (personal communication touchpoints). This is the main rationale behind applying the HOE logic within the ABM for refurbishment.

In previous research, the author developed a HOE model for energetic refurbishment of residential buildings [6]. The resulting model is based on Lewis [7], Lavidge and Steiner [8] and is shown in Figure 1. This model assesses the impact of touchpoints on DM for energetic refurbishment.

The ABM approach simulates decisions and/or behavior of different individual agents. These agents can interact with their environment, as well as with each other. Within an ABM, usually different agents behave according to their individual preferences, their characteristics, their interactions, as well as their environment. Software for ABM allows for the setup and description of different agents, their preferences, interactions, as well as their environment. In this way, the aggregated system with its dynamics (that emerges from many different individual behaviors) can be simulated.

ABM is especially interesting when problems of emergence are studied [9]. This work uses this approach to study refurbishment intention (after interactions with marketing and sales) at a lifestyle and system level.

The last concept described is the Sinus Lifestyle typology. The typology is used in marketing & sales, both in practice and in academics. The Sinus Institute has been monitoring sociocultural developments and trends in the German society since the 1980ies and small adaptations to the lifestyle typology are carried out regularly. The lifestyles are positioned in a two-dimensional space. The x-axis describes their orientation: Traditional towards progressive lifestyles. The y-axis describes social status: Lower class towards upper class.

Ten lifestyles are located within this two-dimensional space. Previous research by the author [6] showed that depending on the Sinus lifestyle, German homeowners have very diverse attitudes and behaviors concerning energetic refurbishment of residential housing. This work uses the Sinus lifestyle approach as it forms an efficient segmentation approach to create differentiated, empirically grounded, agents within the ABM.

Figure 1. Hierarchy of effect model for energetic refurbishment [6]

After this brief description of the key concepts of this paper, the following section will provide a detailed description of the ABM that was developed to simulate the impact of marketing and sales on homeowner's refurbishment decisions.

III. ABM FOR REFURBISHMENT

The ABM for refurbishment is based on empirical data, taken from [6] as displayed in Table 1. The representative sample (n = 4,471) describes the status quo of the DM concerning energetic refurbishment of 17 mi. homeowners in Germany.

It comprises Sinus lifestyle [10] data and their status quo concerning the DM process in the format of the developed HOE model as described in the previous section.

As an example, the adaptive pragmatic lifestyle (with 22.4% behavioral intention) is more than two times as likely to invest in energetic refurbishment compared to the precarious lifestyle (9.3% behavioral intention).

With the help of this data, conversion rates (CR) can be calculated, e.g., 65% of the social ecological lifestyle is converted from knowledge (80.0%) to attitude (52.3%).

Within the ABM for refurbishment, 17,000 agents (homeowners) are set up according to the distribution of the status quo in their refurbishment DM (as displayed in Table 1) and taking into account the real sizes of the ten Sinus lifestyles in German society.

The impact of touchpoints on each individual agent's DM concerning energetic refurbishment is simulated with the HOE model. As a result of the interaction with various touchpoints an agent is guided through the five steps of the HOE model (see Figure 1). Taking one step within the HOE model is calculated with the help of a threshold variable. It is assumed that an agent's threshold variable needs to reach a value of 4, prior to being transferred to the next step in the HOE model. Each touchpoint is increasing the threshold variable with a specific amount. Once an agent has been transferred, the threshold variable is set to 0 again. During the initialization of the model, the threshold variable is set randomly between 0 and 3. Each year, every agent's threshold variable is updated as a result of being exposed to (different) touchpoints.

How much a specific touchpoint increases the threshold variable depends on the touchpoint itself. Touchpoints exist in many appearances and should not be generalized. Not every touchpoint generates the same impact. It is generally acknowledged in marketing and sales, that Mass Communication (MC) touchpoints (e.g., advertising campaigns and information brochures) are best suitable to transfer consumers through the first stages of DM, especially awareness, but as well knowledge and to a lesser extend interest. Furthermore, Personal Communication (PC) touchpoints (e.g., sales talks) are generally more suitable to transfer consumers through the last stages of DM, especially intention, but as well conviction and to a lesser extend interest [11][12].

TABLE I. EMPIRICAL DATA FROM [6]

German's Sinus lifestyle	Status quo in DM				
	Aware -ness [%]	Know-ledge [%]	Atti-tude [%]	Con-viction [%]	Inten-tion [%]
Homeowners in general	98.7	77.1	48.5	33.5	14.3
1. Established conservat.	99.0	80.1	51.0	33.7	14.9
2. Liberal-intellectual	99.7	82.9	57.9	40.6	13.3
3. High achiever	98.9	79.5	48.4	32.9	18.4
4. Movers and shakers	98.4	76.9	52.3	34.6	16.6
5. Adaptive pragmatics	99.5	69.0	53.9	42.4	22.4
6. Social-ecological	99.7	80,0	52.3	36.2	17.0
7. New middle class	98.5	76.9	44.1	32.6	11.8
8. Traditional	99.0	78.8	44.5	30.8	10.6
9. Precarious	99.6	64.4	36.1	20.6	9.3
10. Escapists	92.8	59.3	33.7	21.9	12.2

In the specific case of energetic refurbishment, homeowner have varying informational needs. In the first stages of DM there is usually a stronger focus on information gathering. In the later stages of DM, an interaction is usually necessary, to assess and to judge different financial, technical, or constructional aspects of the energetic refurbishment [13]-[15]. Especially these informational needs cannot be satisfied by mass communication alone.

So, mass communication can unfold a full impact in the beginning, but no impact at the end of the DM process. Personal communication can unfold a full impact at the end, but no impact in the beginning of the DM process.

This phenomenon is reflected in the model by incorporating a correction factor (CF) for the additions to the threshold variable. The correction factor for mass communication (CF_{MC}) is decreasing for every consecutive step (1.0; 0,5; 0.0 and 0.0) and the correction factor for personal communication (CF_{PC}) is increasing for every consecutive step (0.0; 0.0; 0.5 and 1.0) in the DM process. These values of the correction factors at specific stages of DM are assumed. Finally, every agent's threshold variable is increased with a value as shown in (1) in each period.

$$(CR * MC * CF_{MC}) + (CR * PC * CF_{PC}) \quad (1)$$

Equation (1) incorporates the variables MC as well as PC, which stand for Mass Communication (MC) and Personal Communication (PC). During the initializations of the model, these variables can be set equal to the amount of mass and personal communication that the agents is exposed to during one period (of the simulation).

The amount of mass communication has a range between 0 and 5, which means that a homeowner is exposed to one mass communication touchpoint (e.g., a television or a radio commercial or an online advertising) between 0 (no exposure) and 5 times in one period. The amount of personal communication has a range of 0 to 5 as well. The meaning of this personal communication touchpoint range is linked to the number of energy consultants that is available and active. Currently, approx. 15,000 to 30,000 energy consultants for residential buildings are active in Germany, depending on the used definitions [16][17]. They realized approx. 280,000 energy consultancy reports in 2022 (compared to approx. 180,000 reports in 2021 and 100,000 reports in 2020 [18][19]). Such an energy consultancy report is assumably the result of a series of five personal communication touchpoints (e.g., personal emails and phone calls and visits). So, 30,000 energy consultants realized 1.4 mi. personal communication touch points in 2022. This paper assumes that 30,000 energy consultants could realize a maximum of 3 mi. personal communication touchpoints, leading to a maximum of 600,000 energy consultancy reports per period, in the years to come. This maximum practically means doubling their output in terms of personal communication touchpoints, compared to already high 2022 levels.

Section I described that in the past, governments mainly campaigned to push refurbishment. This can now be simulated with, e.g., MC = 5 and PC = 0. More recently, (local) governments have been offering and facilitating personal visits and consultancy by energy consultants in a limited way, which can be seen as a sales measure. This can now be simulated with, e.g., MC = 5 and PC = 1. The impact of any mix of marketing and sales measures can now be simulated by the model.

Section I mentioned as well that some ABM include social influence to simulate DM in a context of energy transition. Baranzini et al. investigated social influence in photovoltaic panel diffusion in Switzerland and conclude that "Social contagion is also a driver of adoptions in the private sector". They add "We also confirm [...] that social contagion is a very localized and short-term phenomenon, whose strength declines with distance and time." [20]. The ABM for refurbishment incorporates this phenomenon in the following way. Each positive refurbishment decision in the direct neighborhood of an agent leads to an acceleration of the DM process. This is implemented in the model by increasing the threshold variable by 30% for every neighboring agent's positive refurbishment, as shown in (2).

$$(100\% + (\text{No. of agents} * 30\%)) \quad (2)$$

Potentially, the acceleration can reach multiples of 30%. The maximum acceleration however is set to 120% (because of 4 neighboring agents, or more than 4 neighboring agents, taking positive refurbishment decisions). This acceleration effect is limited to two periods after the period of the refurbishment. In the model 5,041 districts with 17,000 homeowners exist. Each district has an average of 3,4 homeowners.

Another essential aspect of touchpoints is their price. In general, mass communication is less costly than personal communication. A common way to quote prices in mass media is with the help of the costs per mille (CPM) metric, which expresses the price per 1,000 views. Price ranges for CPM vary greatly, as media vary greatly in type and quality. An average CPM for mass media in the ABM for refurbishment is set to € 13.50. This is based on a media mix of Television (30 seconds advertisement, median $ 36 CPM), Radio (30 seconds advertisement, median $ 6.75 CPM), Online (300 x 250 banner ad, median $ 2.27 CPM) and magazines (full page color ad, median $13.24 CPM) [21]. US-Dollar ($) to Euro (€) conversion done on the 25th of August 2023. The costs for a personal communication touchpoint in the ABM for refurbishment is set to € 16.67. It is assumed that a salesperson costs € 80,000 per year and has 200 working days per year. During a typical 5-day work week in average of 16 potential customers can be visited. Furthermore, during each working day, 10 phone calls and 10 Emails can be processed. This leads to 4,800 touch points, or € 16.67 per touchpoint.

An optimization of refurbishment intention and costs is not sufficient, as the speed of refurbishment needs to increase (see Section I). As time is an importance factor, this paper limits the modeling time to 27 years (2023 to 2050) and tries to identify the costs for more refurbishment speed.

Finally, it must be mentioned that the ABM for refurbishment was realized in the Netlogo environment [22]. The model's code is available under GitHub [23]. The simulation results were imported in Microsoft Excel to analyze and plot them.

IV. RESULTS AND DISCUSSION

This section presents and discusses the results of the ABM for refurbishment. First, the impact of different levels of mass and personal communication over a fixed period of 27 years (from 2023 – 2050) are investigated. Therefore, a first sample was created that consists of 720 observations (n = 720). One observation is the result of running the ABM for refurbishment 27 years. 20 observations were done for every combination of Mass Communication (MC) and Personal Communication (PC) between 0 and 5 (see Section III), to account for stochasticity in the model. Second, this paper looks into the velocity of developing refurbishment intention, for which a second sample is created. This sample consists again of 720 observations (n = 720), however, the ABM for refurbishment only runs until a refurbishment intention of 95% among homeowners is reached. With specific combinations of mass and personal communication, this happens in less than 27 years. Both samples documented all homeowner's reached status quo in the DM process. Furthermore, the costs that are involved with mass and personal communication are recorded, as well as Sinus lifestyle data. Analysis shows that the first and the second sample do not differ significantly for these key variables.

Figure 2 shows the impact of mass and personal communication on refurbishment intention at an overall system level after 27 years (sample I). One important finding is that mass communication alone does not convince homeowners to refurbish. This modeling result is in line with the previously described phenomenon that governments mainly used mass communication in the past and could hardly change the hesitant refurbishment behavior of German homeowners. The portion of homeowners with a refurbishment intention increases from 14.3% (see Table I) to 18.6% after 27 years of mass communication. This result can be interpreted as a indicator that governments have been working cost inefficiently by investing solely in mass communication campaigns.

The costs for mass and personal communications are illustrated in Figure 3. These are accumulated economic costs after a fixed period of 27 years of mass and personal communication exposure. Later in this paper, specific mixes of

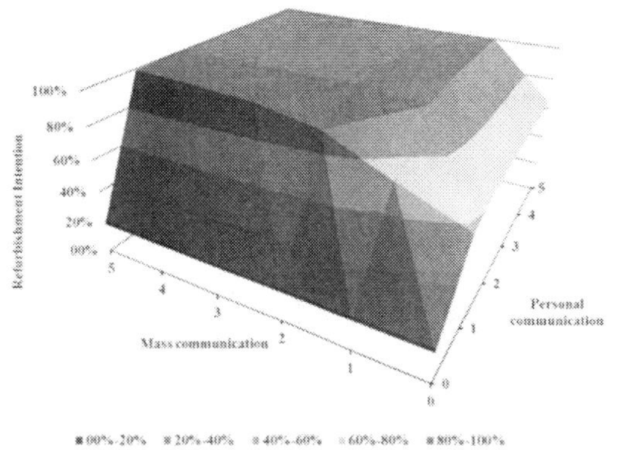

Figure 2. Mass and personal communication and refurbishment intention

mass and personal communication will be identified that enable an acceleration of the creation of refurbishment intention and less time than the fixed period of 27 years will be necessary, resulting in lower economic costs.

Figure 3 shows that personal communication is the main driver of total costs. And it is important to acknowledge that these accumulated costs represent the economic costs and are not necessarily paid by one and the same party. This makes them abstract and somehow intangible. While governments might invest in mass communication campaigns, households might invest in energy consultancy. Nevertheless, an optimal point should be identified, where all (or most) homeowners decide to refurbish at least costs. This point can be identified at MC = 5 and PC = 1. At this point, the model shows that after 27 years, 99.2% of German homeowners developed a refurbishment intention at economic costs of € 301.01 mi.

In a next step, this paper investigates the velocity of developing a refurbishment intention of 95% among homeowners, with the help of sample II. This seems a highly relevant information, as it could reveal levels of mass and personal communication that convince homeowners to refurbish more rapidly. In this way the model can determine the additional costs for more rapid refurbishment paths. The cost in Figure 3 should now be adjusted as well, as with specific mixes of mass and personal communication, less than 27 years are necessary to reach a 95% refurbishment intention. Figure 5 shows these adjusted total accumulated costs.

The optimal point can be identified for Figure 4 and 5 as well: still at MC = 5 and PC = 1 a 99.2% refurbish intention among Germany's homeowners until the year 2050 is reached (and a 95% refurbish intention is reached slightly earlier in the year 2048). The economic costs would yield up to € 301.01 mi. (at 99.2% in the year 2050) or € 278.7 mi. (at least at 95% refurbishment intention in the year 2048). Faster pathways however are now becoming visible and are listed in Table 2, as well as the additional costs for this acceleration. The additional costs are calculated by comparing the specific scenario with the optimal point MC = 5 and PC = 1. The table is sorted by the column duration in years and shows the levels of mass and personal communication (MC and PC) that reach a 95% refurbishment intention.

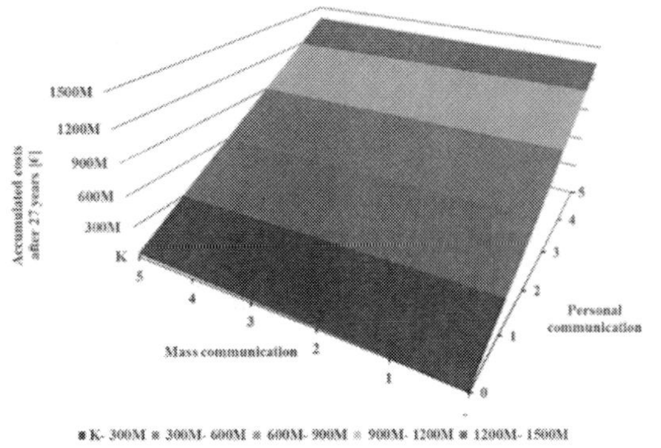

Figure 3. Total costs of communication after 27 years

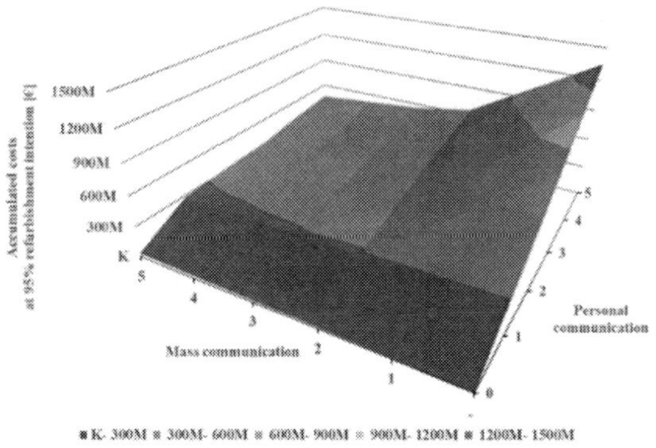

Figure 5. Total costs of communication at 95% refurbishment intention

As an example, the duration of developing a refurbishment intention of 95% among German homeowners can be reduced by 10 years by looking at the MC = 5 and PC = 2. With these levels of mass and personal communication, the system reaches a 95% refurbishment intention after 15 years with additional costs of € 38.6 mi. Practically, this means additional investments of 89% per year (€ 278.7 mi. over 27 years compared to € 317.3 mi. over 15 years), or 14% over the whole period. Another example is the point MC = 3 and PC = 2 at which a 95% refurbishment intention is reached after 17 years (instead of 25 years) with additional costs of € 73.1 mi. Practically, this means additional investments of 86% per year (€ 278.7 mi. in 25 years compared to € 351.8 mi. in 17 years), or 26% over the whole period.

V. Conclusion and Future Work

The ABM for refurbishment and the results in this paper investigate the research question whether there are optimal (cost efficient and concerning speed) mixes of marketing and sales measures that help homeowners to create a positive refurbishment intention. To answer this research question model based, an ABM model for refurbishment is developed that utilizes (for German homeowners) representative data concerning their DM process for energetic refurbishment.

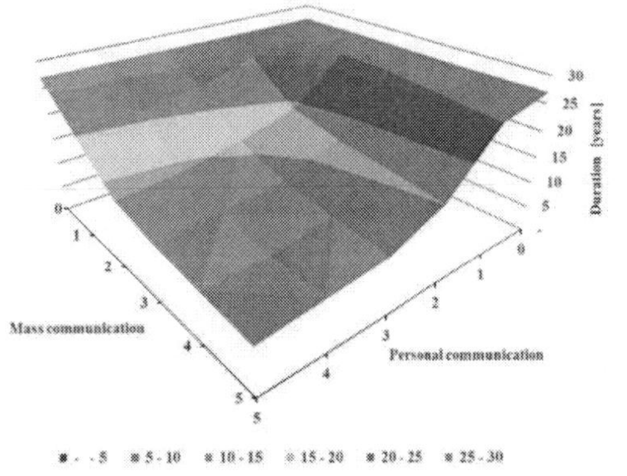

Figure 4. Time duration of reaching a 95% refurbishment intention

This paper describes different samples that were created for the two different sub questions. The ABM for refurbishment shows that advanced levels of Mass Communication (MC = 5) and small to moderate levels (PC = 1) of Personal Communication can lead to a refurbishment intention saturation among German homeowners in a cost-efficient way. This result suggests that past initiatives from governments to create refurbishment intention through mass communication only were inefficient. This paper explores as well additional costs for an acceleration of the development of refurbishment intention under the influence of mass and personal communication. Even if the economic costs estimated in this paper seem somehow abstract and intangible, the model shows that specific levels of mass and personal communication can significantly accelerate the creation of refurbishment intention in the population at accumulated costs that do not seem unfeasible. The explorations in this paper show that there is a potential to speed up the energy transition in buildings.

TABLE II. ADDITIONAL COSTS FOR FASTER REFURBISHMENT

Combinations of MC and PC		Characteristics of combination		
MC	PC	Duration [years]	Accumulated costs [mi. €]	Additional costs vs. MC = 5 / PC = 1[mi. €]
5	5	9	460.4	181.7
4	4	10	409.3	130.6
5	4	10	411.6	132.9
4	5	10	509.3	230.6
5	3	11	342.7	64.0
3	5	11	557.4	278.7
4	3	12	371.1	92.4
3	4	12	488.4	209.7
3	3	13	399.0	120.3
2	5	13	656.1	377.4
2	4	14	566.0	287.3
5	2	15	317.3	38.6
4	2	16	334.8	56.1
2	3	16	487.4	208.7
3	2	17	351.8	73.1
2	2	19	388.8	110.1
1	5	20	1,004.8	726.1
1	4	21	845.0	566.3
1	3	23	696.4	417.7
1	2	26	526.7	248.0

This paper does without an explicit sensitivity analysis for the ABM for refurbishment, as the explorations discussed in this paper represent a kind of sensitivity analysis for refurbishment intention among homeowners by itself. This paper presents different figures (e.g., Figure 2 and 4), which assess the sensitivity of refurbishment intention (in terms of the portion of homeowners with refurbishment intention, and in terms of the time to develop this refurbishment intention) as a result of different mass and personal communication levels.

Although this work develops a segmented approach to simulating German homeowners' DM for energetic refurbishment, it assesses the costs for touchpoints for these homeowners in a lump-sum kind of way at the end of Section III. Future work could address this issue and do an attempt to develop a segmented and more realistic cost calculation approach for the different Sinus Lifestyles.

Another issue lies in the simulation of specific (but static) mixes of mass and personal communication over a longer period. It is common marketing practice to vary campaigns over time, which is not incorporated in the ABM for refurbishment. Future versions should dynamize the levels of mass and personal communication over time (within the simulation time of 27 years, e.g., reducing mass communication from MC = 5 to MC = 1 and increasing personal communication from PC = 0 to PC = 1 over time).

The same holds for the static approach concerning the capacities of energy consultants. Section III discusses a maximum of 3 mi. personal communication touchpoints per period, in the years to come. Most likely, capacity will increase in case of change of momentum in the refurbishment market and this should be considered in the model.

REFERENCES

[1] M. Verhoog, "Steuerung von Akteuren und Entscheidungen in Baunetzwerken [in English: Controlling Actors and Decisions in Construction Networks]", Springer Gabler, Wiesbaden, 2018, ISBN 978-3658205867.

[2] M. Verhoog, "Optimal Usage of Marketing and Sales to Push Residential Refurbishment", SIMUL 2022, IARIA, pp. 35-37, ISBN: 978-1685580018.

[3] H. Du, Q. Han, and B. de Vries, "Modelling Energy-Efficient Renovation Adoption and Diffusion Process for Households: a Review and a Way Forward, in: Sustainable Cities and Society, Vol. 77, pp. 1-10, 2022, https://doi.org/10.1016/j.scs.2021.103560.

[4] W. Jager, "The four P's in Social Simulation, a Perspective on how Marketing could benefit from the Use of Social Simulation", in: Journal of Business Research, Vol. 60, Issue 8, pp. 868–875, 2007, https://doi.org/10.1016/j.jbusres.2007.02.003.

[5] S. A. Delre, W. Jager, T. H. A. Bijmolt and M. A. Janssen, "Targeting and Timing Promotional activities: An Agent-based Model for the Takeoff of New Products" in: Journal of Business Research, Vol. 60, Issue 8, pp. 826–835, 2007, https://doi.org/10.1016/j.jbusres.2007.02.002.

[6] M. Verhoog, "A Target Group-specific Communication Approach to Push Refurbishment", Energy for Sustainability International Conference, Funchal, 2017.

[7] T. Barry, "The Development of the Hierarchy of Effects: An Historical Perspective", in: Current Issues & Research in Advertising, Vol. 10, Issue 2, pp. 251-295, 1987, DOI: 10.1080/01633392.1987.10504921.

[8] R. Lavidge and G. Steiner, "A Model For Predictive Measurements of Advertising Effectiveness.", in: Journal of Marketing 25, pp. 59-62, 1961, https://doi.org/10.1177/002224296102500611.

[9] S. Railsback and V. Grimm, "Agent-Based and Individual-Based Modeling", University Press, Princeton, 2012, ISBN 978-0691136745.

[10] Sinus Institut, "What are Sinus-Milieus?", 2023, https://www.sinus-institut.de/en/sinus-milieus (accessed: 27th of October 2023).

[11] P. de Pelsmacker, M. Geuens and J. Van den Bergh, "Marketing communications", 6th edition, Pearson Education, Harlow, 2017, ISBN 978-1292135762.

[12] P. Kotler and K. Keller, "Marketing Management", 13th edition, Pearson Prentice Hall, Upper Saddle River, 2009, ISBN 978-0131357976.

[13] C. Maby et al., "Energy Advice in Europe 2007: A review of current practice in advice on sustainable energy in countries of the European Union", European Commission, 2007.

[14] R. Schüle, A. Bierwirth and T. Madry, „Zukunft der Energieberatung in Deutschland [in English: The Future of Energy Efficiency Consultancy in Germany]", Wüstenrot Stiftung, Ludwigsburg, 2011, ISBN 978-3933249760.

[15] E. Dunkelberg and I. Stieß, „Energieberatung für Eigenheimbesitzer/innen, Wege zur Verbesserung von Bekanntheit und Transparenz durch Systematisierung, Qualitätssicherung und kommunale Vernetzung [in English: Energy Efficiency Consultancy for Homeowners, How to improve Awareness and Transparency through Systematization, Quality Assurance and Communal Networking]", Institut für ökologische Wirtschaftsforschung IÖW, Berlin, 2011.

[16] Bundesverband GIH, "Analyse des Energieberatungsmarktes 2019 veröffentlicht [in English: Analysis of Energy Consultancy Market 2019 published]", Berlin, 2021.

[17] Frankfurter Allgemeine Zeitung FAZ and H. Rampe, "Verloren im Expertendschungel [in English: Lost in the jungle of experts]", 2020, in: https://www.faz.net/aktuell/-wirtschaft/wohnen/bauen/wie-findet-man-den-passenden-energieberater-16647176/den-waermebruecken-mit-der-16661816.html (accessed: 27th of October 2023).

[18] Deutsche Energie Effizienz Agentur DEEA, "Zahl der Energieberatungen sprunghaft gestiegen [in English: Jump in number of Energy Consultancies]", 2023, https://deea.de/2023/01/26/zahl-der-energieberatungen-sprunghaft-gestiegen/ (accessed: 27th of October 2023).

[19] Zeit online, "Zahl der Energieberatungen um 100.000 gestiegen [in English: Number of Energy Consulties went up by 100,000], 2023, in: https://www.zeit.de/wirtschaft/2023-01/energiekrise-energieberatung-verbraucherzentrale-anstieg (accessed: 27th of October 2023).

[20] A. Baranzini, S. Carattini and M. Pécla, "What drives Social Contagion in the Adoption of Solar Photovoltaic Technology?", GRI Working Papers 270, Grantham Research Institute on Climate Change and the Environment, 2017.

[21] Solomon Partners, "Media Monthly", 2021, in: https://solomonpartners.com/wp-content/uploads/2021/10/-Solomon-Partners-Media-Monthly-October-2021.pdf (accessed: 27th of October 2023).

[22] U. Wilensky, "Netlogo", http://ccl.northwestern.edu/netlogo/. Center for Connected Learning and Computer-Based Modeling, Northwestern University, Evanston, IL, 1999.

[23] Please refer to Github under https://github.com/mart-verhoog/marketing-and-sales-to-push-residential-refurbishment.git for all code in the NetLogo environment of the ABM for refurbishment.

Security Process for Adopting Machine to Machine Communication for Maintenance in Transportation with a Focus on Key Establishment

Sibylle Fröschle
Institute for Secure Cyber-Physical Systems
Hamburg University of Technology
Hamburg, Germany
sibylle.froeschle(at)tuhh.de

Martin Kubisch
Airbus CRT
Munich, Germany
martin.kubisch(at)airbus.com

***Abstract*—Machine to machine communication over wireless networks is increasingly adopted to improve service and maintenance processes in transportation, e.g. at airports, ports, and automotive service stations. This brings with it the challenge of how to set up a session key so that the communication can be cryptographically secured. While there is a vast design space of key establishment methods available, there is a lack of process of how to engineer a solution while considering both security and safety: how to assess the threats and risks that come with a particular key establishment method? And how to iteratively refine a key establishment method under development such that risk is mitigated to an acceptable level? In this paper, we put forward an approach that addresses these questions. Moreover, we illustrate our approach by means of a real-world use case: TAGA — a Touch and Go Assistant in the Aerospace Domain. Finally, we highlight the crucial role that simulation has to play in this security process for safety.**

***Index Terms*—security, simulation, threat and risk analysis, transportation**

I. Introduction

Machine to Machine (M2M) communication over wireless networks is increasingly adopted to improve service and maintenance processes in transportation, e.g. at airports, ports, and automotive service stations. This does not come without security challenges: often these processes are safety-critical, and often, attacks against them would disrupt critical infrastructures. One example are the ground processes at an airport. When an aircraft has landed and reached its parking slot at the apron many processes such as refuelling and pre-conditioning are performed. M2M communication between the aircraft and the respective ground unit allow us to optimize these processes with respect to accuracy of service, energy-efficiency, safety, and time. The aircraft will send sensor values (e.g. temperature or fuel readings), and the ground unit can adopt flow parameters accordingly. It is clear that if an attacker managed to spoof fake sensor values into the M2M communication then this could compromise safety.

The adoption of M2M communication brings with it the challenge of how to set up a session key so that the communication can be cryptographically secured. The state of the art of key establishment offers two approaches: either we can

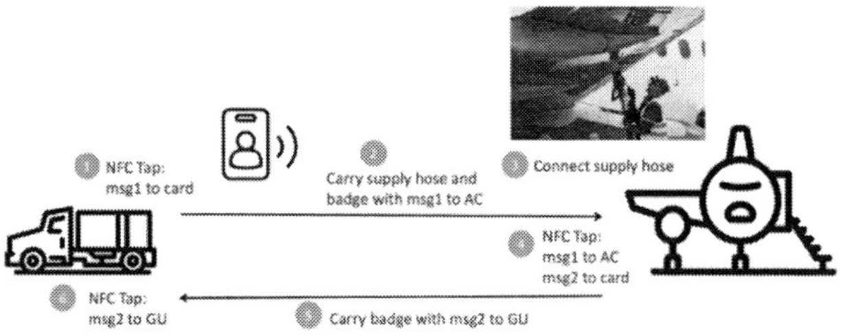

Fig. 1. Pairing up a ground unit and an airplane

make use of an *authenticated key establishment protocol* [1] but have to deal with the challenge of how to securely set up and manage a pre-shared security context. Or, we can try to translate the idea of *secure device pairing* [2]–[4] into our context of safety-critical machines.

To adopt M2M communication for ground processes at airports a *touch and go assistant in the aerospace domain (TAGA)* is currently under development. Each aircraft and ground unit is equipped with a TAGA controller that contains a secure element for cryptographic operations and a Near Field Communication (NFC) reader. Moreover, the operator of each ground unit is provided with a passive NFC card. Altogether, this allows them to transport messages for key establishment from the ground unit to the aircraft, and back by means of taps with the NFC card against the respective NFC reader. The 'TAGA walk' can conveniently be integrated into the operator's usual path to the aircraft and back while connecting up the respective supply hose. This is illustrated in Fig. 1.

Integrating M2M communication in transportation has to undergo a safety and security engineering process conform to the safety and security norms applicable to the respective domain (such as ISO/SAE 21434 for road vehicles and DO-178C, DO-254, DO-326A and ARP4754 in the aeronautics domain). This process will typically involve the following activities. First, vulnerable assets have to be identified (such as here the communication channel). Second, for each asset the potential threats have to be collected (e.g. by a keyword-guided method such as STRIDE). And third, for each threat a risk level has to be determined. The risk level is typically determined by, on the one hand, rating the safety impact of the threat, and, on the other hand, rating the likelihood that the threat can be implemented. As a result, the risk level will decide whether protection by security controls is required, and to which assurance level the corresponding security requirements have to be validated.

When it comes to integrating security controls and security systems the most relevant and widely adopted standard is Common Criteria (CC) (ISO/IEC 15408). This standard allows us to define a profile of security requirements for a target of evaluation that fall into security functional requirements, and assurance requirements. The latter specify that the security functional requiremens must be validated to a sufficient assurance level. While a CC profile provides a clear interface between safety and security this should not be taken as an excuse to stop short of a stronger integration between security and safety engineering. Without it important safety measures that can mitigate security risks might be overlooked.

Problem and Contribution: To sum up, while there is a vast design space of key establishment methods available, some of them with CC evaluation, there is a lack of process of how to engineer a solution while integrating both security and safety: how to assess the threats and risks that come with a particular key establishment method in a specific context? And how to iteratively refine a key establishment method under development such that risk is mitigated to an acceptable level? In this paper, we put forward and illustrate an approach that addresses these questions.

In Section II we motivate and present our overall approach. Our approach is based on the concept of *connection compromise states*, which define how key establishment can fail, and provide a finer-grained interface between security and safety. In Section III we motivate and illustrate our approach by means of the TAGA use case. In Section IV we give a workflow on how to assess and mitigate the safety impact starting from the connection compromise states. In particular, we highlight the important role of simulation in this workflow. In Section V we draw conclusions and discuss future work.

II. Key Establishment for Vehicle to Service Unit Communication

Setting: We first define the problem setting. As shown by example in Fig. 1 we assume that there is a vehicle V that is to undergo a maintenance procedure at some location. The maintenance procedure can involve several types of services, and each service involves at least one service unit. Each service unit is either directly coupled to the vehicle (e.g. via a supply hose) or indirectly (e.g. via the loading of goods). To optimize the maintenance procedure each service unit shall be able to engage in M2M communication with the vehicle it services: to exchange data such as sensor and status values or even instructions on how to move. Several such procedures can take place in parallel in adjacent or remote locations.

TABLE I
SECURITY REQUIREMENTS FOR V2SU KEY ESTABLISHMENT

1)	*Secrecy of the session key.* Upon completion of the key establishment method, the service unit and the vehicle should have established a session key which is known to the vehicle and service unit only.
2)	*Uniqueness of the session key.* Each run of the key establishment method should produce distinct, independent session keys.
3)	*Service unit authentication.* Upon completion of the key establishment method, if a vehicle believes it is communicating with a service unit on the session with key k and parameters $p_1, \ldots, p_n$ then there is indeed an authentic service unit that is executing a session with key k and parameters $p_1, \ldots, p_n$.
4)	*Vehicle authentication.* Upon completion of the key establishment method, if a service unit believes it is communicating with a vehicle on the session with key k and parameters $p_1, \ldots, p_n$ then there is indeed an authentic vehicle that is executing a session with key k and parameters $p_1, \ldots, p_n$.
5)	*Agreement with physical setup.* Upon completion of the key establishment method, the service unit and vehicle should also be linked by the respective physical setup.

We assume that the communication is conducted over a wireless channel (such as Wi-Fi IEEE 802.11), and that a corresponding protocol to ensure data confidentiality and integrity during data transmission is already determined (such as AES-GCM for Wi-Fi IEEE 802.11). Here we focus on the challenge of how to establish the necessary session key between a service unit and the vehicle.

Security Requirements: Table I shows the security properties that any key establishment method for Vehicle to Service Unit (V2SU) communication must at least satisfy. Properties (1) and (2) ensure that the key remains secret, and that it is fresh for each session. Properties (3) and (4) are derived from the standard authentication properties for key establishment protocols [5]. We have formulated the properties without explicitly referring to the names of the peers. This is to allow for secure device pairing as the key establishment method of choice. Names can, however, be included in the parameter list. One can also include the type of service, and other service specific parameters into the parameter list. Property (5) is specific to our setting: it ensures that the cyber channel indeed connects the machines that are physically coupled in the maintenance service.

Design Space: The state of the art of key establishment offers two approaches to achieve the secrecy and authentication properties: one is to employ an *Authenticated Key Establishment (AKE) Protocol* [1]; the second is to make use of a *Secure Device Pairing (SDP) scheme* [4]. As we will see later a combination is also possible.

AKE protocols [1] are by now well-investigated, and there exist many standardized protocols that come with formal security proofs. One example is the handshake protocol of Transport Layer Security (TLS). The advantage of AKE protocols is that they are designed to be secure in the presence of active adversaries: their security proofs assume an attacker who has complete control of the network. The drawback is that communication partners need to pre-share a security context such as a pre-shared long-term secret or a public key infrastructure. This typically results in a key management overhead, which can in turn be the source of further threats to the system.

SDP [4] schemes make do without a pre-shared security context but instead rely on so-called Out-of-Band (OoB) channels to safeguard against man-in-the-middle attacks. These schemes have been widely adopted for Internet of Things (IoT) and personal devices. One example is Bluetooth pairing of a device to one's smartphone. Often the human user is used as the OoB channel; other schemes make use of properties of wireless channels such as Near Field Communication (NFC). The challenge is that the OoB channel must provide authenticity, and it is not always possible to validate this to a high assurance level: e.g. because a human user is involved or because it is difficult to establish that the wireless channel indeed satisfies authenticity. The great advantage of SDP in our context is that it makes do without a pre-established security context. Moreover, it will help us to achieve Property (5): to pair up two devices typically comes with proximity or some physical interaction, and in our context this can be woven into the procedure of the physical setup of the two machines.

Security Engineering for Safety: How to assess the threats and risks that come with a particular key establishment method in our context? And how to iteratively refine a key establishment method under development such that risk is mitigated to an acceptable level? At first sight, one might be tempted to proceed as follows: assess the safety impact when the key establishment method maximally fails (i.e. when the attacker has full control over the connection); derive a safety level, and translate this into a Common Criteria security assurance level; hand this over to a company that provides key establishment products; and acquire a product with the corresponding Common Criteria certificate.

However, this approach has the drawback that it closes the door to measures on the cyber-physical service itself, and hence, to measures that mitigate the safety impact directly. Moreover, in our context where actors come from different security domains we cannot exclude insider attacks, and hence, this approach might overlook some threats that cannot be reduced in their likelihood by even the highest assurance level.

Instead, we wish to reflect that a successful attack against a key establishment method can have different outcomes, and that certain outcomes might be easier to achieve for the attacker than others. To this end, we identify in which ways a supposedly secure connection can be compromised following a breach of the key establishment method. The resulting *connection compromise states* are described in Table II and illustrated in Fig. 2. The security engineering activities can now be carried out in a structured and systematic fashion as follows:

1) The security experts identify the threats against the key establishment method under investigation, and assess for each connection compromise state the likelihood that this state can be reached by an attacker.

TABLE II
CONNECTION COMPROMISE STATES FOLLOWING A BREACH OF V2SU KEY ESTABLISHMENT

1)	*Man-in-the-middle (MitM).* The service unit has a connection secured by session key K and the vehicle has a connection secured by key K' but the attacker knows both K and K'.
2)	*Impersonation to service unit (Imp2SU).* The service unit has a connection secured by session key K but the attacker knows K.
3)	*Impersonation to vehicle (Imp2V).* The vehicle has a connection secured by session key K but the attacker knows K.
4)	*Parameter mismatch.* A peer has a connection secured by session key K and for a session with parameters $p_1, \ldots, p_n$, and another peer has a connection secured also by K and for a session with parameters $p'_1, \ldots, p'_n$, and the attacker does not know K, but there is $i \in [1, n]$ such that $p_i \neq p'_i$.
5)	*Mismatch with physical setup:* A peer P shares a connection secured by key K with another peer P', and the attacker does not know K, but P and P' are not linked by the respective physical setup.

2) The safety and process engineers of the vehicle and the maintenance procedure assess for each connection compromise state what the severity of impact on safety (and perhaps other factors) will be if the attacker manages to reach this state. Moreover, they explore whether and how the impact can be mitigated by process measures.
3) At synchronization points safety and security experts together decide whether the combination of the current assessments of threat likelihood and safety impact result in an acceptable risk level. If not the workflow will be repeated in an iterative fashion until an optimal solution is reached. Finally, assurance levels for the security components and the mitigation safety measures will be derived, and forwarded for development, or product integration respectively.

We will discuss a workflow for the activities of Part (2) in more detail in Section IV since this is where simulation plays a crucial role throughout. Part (1) will only be illustrated via our case study. Here simulation might also play an important role, e.g. to analyse channel properties with respect to a SDP scheme. For a detailed analysis we employ the tools for formal protocol verification, such as the Tamarin Protocol Verifier [6].

III. TAGA: A Touch and Go Assistant in the Aerospace Domain

A. The TAGA Protoype

The TAGA Pairing Process: The prototype of TAGA pairing is based on an unauthenticated three-pass key establishment protocol, where the third pass is a key confirmation step. It is illustrated in Fig. 3 for the case when the Diffie-Hellman (DH) key exchange is used as the underlying protocol.

The operator performs a first NFC tap at the ground unit. Thereby a first message M_1 is written to the card. M_1 contains information necessary for establishing the key together with the ID of the ground unit and the service that it provides. Then the operator walks to the aircraft. Typically he will also carry a supply hose; e.g. for pre-conditioning he will carry the air supply hose.

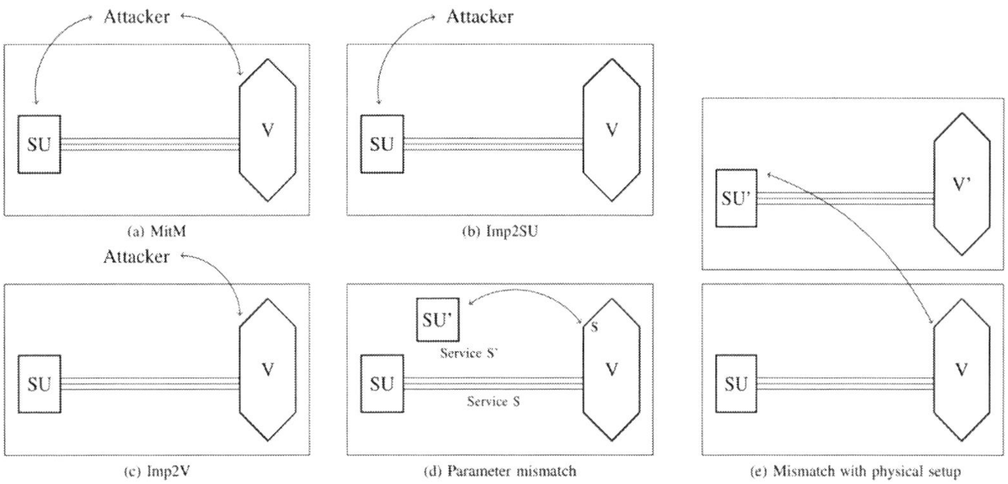

Fig. 2. Illustration of the connection compromise states

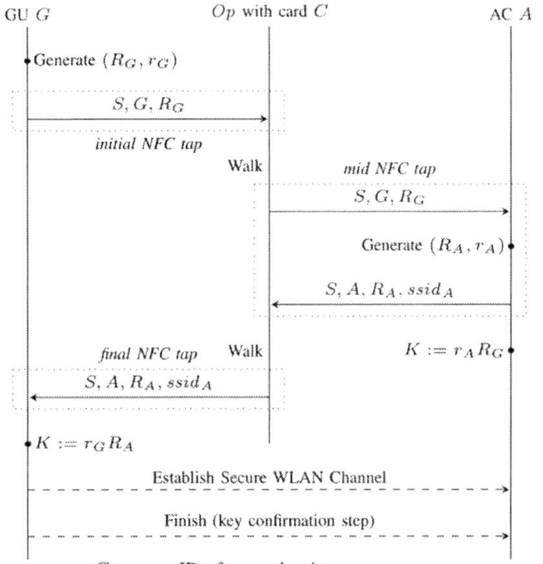

G	ID of ground unit
A	ID of aircraft
S	service name of ground unit
$ssid_A$	SSID of the aircraft's WLAN
R_G, r_G	public and private DH key of G
R_A, r_A	public and private DH key of A
K	resulting session key

Fig. 3. TAGA pairing with Diffie-Hellman key exchange

At the aircraft, the operator first performs some physical setup, such as connecting the supply hose to the supply port, and then carries out the second NFC tap. Thereby, M_1 is transferred to the aircraft's TAGA controller, and a second message M_2 is written onto the card. M_2 contains information necessary for establishing the key together with the ID of the aircraft and access data to its WLAN such as the SSID. M_2 also contains a ciphertext to grant key confirmation to the ground unit. The operator then walks back to the ground unit.

Back at the ground unit, the operator carries out a final NFC tap, and transfers M_2 to the ground unit's TAGA controller. The ground unit is now able to connect to the aircraft's WLAN. A third message is passed over the WLAN connection to achieve key confirmation to the aircraft. Finally, the operator activates the ground unit; e.g. for pre-conditioning he switches on the air supply. Now the ground unit and the aircraft are ready to carry out the service using M2M communication.

Threats against the TAGA Channel: Even though TAGA takes place in a secure zone, where only authorized personnel have access, our analysis has shown that there are many indirect ways of compromising the authenticity of the TAGA channel. One example is that the attacker might swap a counterfeit card for the TAGA card, e.g. while the operator takes a break. Another example is that the attacker might eavesdrop on the NFC exchange from outside the secure zone of the turnaround, e.g. by using a special antenna to increase the nominal range of NFC.

The following example shows that the combination of card swapping and eavesdropping already allows the attacker to implement the classic man-in-the-middle attack against the basic Diffie-Hellman exchange over the TAGA channel.

Example 1 (MitM by Swap & Eavesdrop). Let A be an aircraft and G be a ground unit at parking slot L so that G is to service A. In preparation, the attacker swaps his own prepped card C_I for the operator's card, e.g. while the operator is on a break. Moreover, the attacker sets up NFC eavesdropping capability, and his own WLAN access point AP_I in the range of L. Both C_I and AP_I are prepped with a fixed DH key pair (r_I, R_I), and the SSID $ssid_I$ of the attacker's WLAN.

The attack then proceeds as depicted in Fig. 4. The card C_I carries out the first tap as usual. However, with the second tap the counterfeit card writes the attacker's public key R_I to A rather than G's public key R_G. Similarly, with the third tap the card writes R_I and $ssid_I$ to G rather than A's public key R_A and SSID $ssid_A$. Hence, G computes session key K_{GI} based on r_G and R_I, and A computes session key K_{IA} based on r_A and R_I.

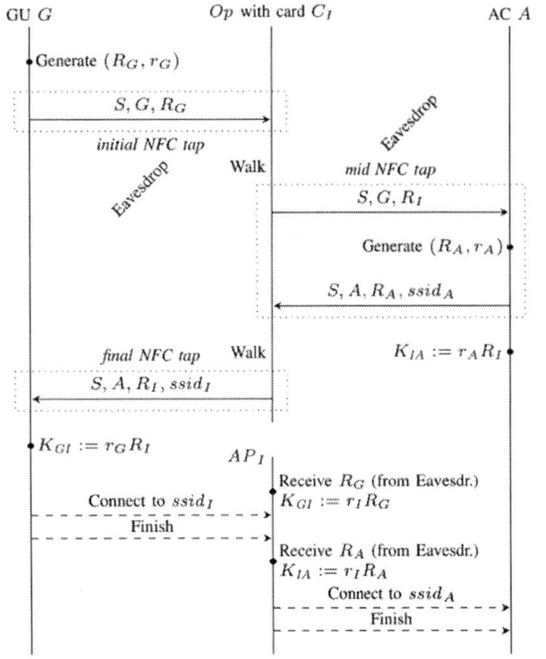

Fig. 4. Man-in-the-middle attack by card swapping and eavesdropping

To be able to compute the same keys the attacker needs to get R_G and R_A onto his access point AP_I. Even if the card only has a passive NFC interface he can use eavesdropping to do so. Once he has computed K_{GI} and K_{IA} he can establish the corresponding channels, and mount a MitM attack against the M2M communication between G and A.

Estimating the Safety Impact: To estimate the severity of impact of a MitM connection compromise we consider the two ground services fuelling and pre-conditioning. Our examples show that while for fuelling the safety impact is controlled by inbuilt safety measures this is not the case for pre-conditioning, and the safety impact is potentially high.

Example 2 (Fuelling). The attacker can forge fuel orders, and induce the fuel truck to load an insufficient or surplus amount of fuel. While this can be highly disruptive there is no safety impact. Since the aircraft measures the fuel itself it will notice if the loaded fuel is not sufficient. Moreover, if the attacker tries to cause spillage (and hence, a fire hazard) by too large a fuel order this will not succeed since the backflow will stop the pump of the fuel truck.

Example 3 (Pre-Conditioning). The attacker can forge airflow parameters and sensor values that will induce the pre-conditioning unit to apply air pressure and temperature unsuitable to the aircraft. This can be highly damaging: if the cooling process is too fast then water in the pipes can quickly become frozen and clog up the pipes. This can happen very quickly: e.g. with the lowest inlet temperature within 30 seconds, with safety considerations still within 100 seconds. The resulting backflow will be detected by the pre-conditioning unit. However, in the worst case pipes might already have burst. In any case the pipes have to be checked for damage afterwards, which is a costly procedure.

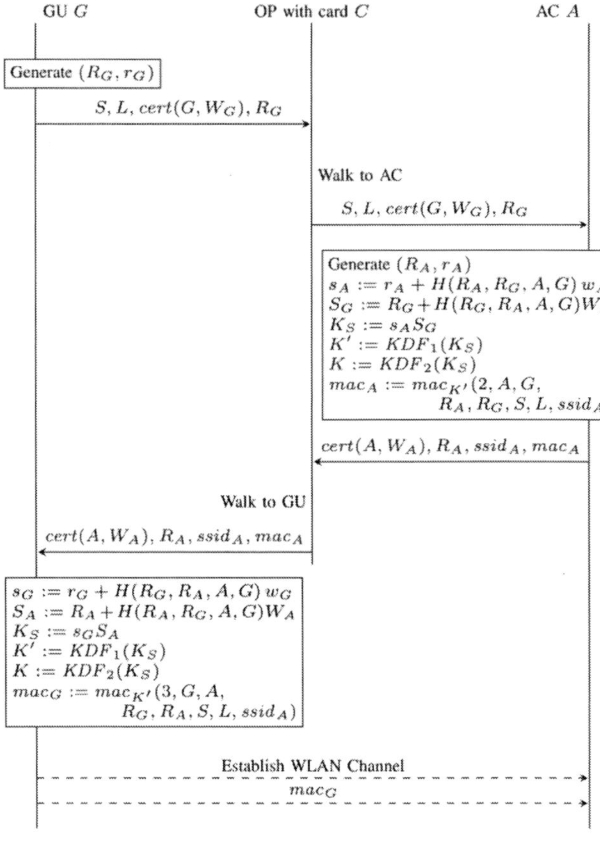

Fig. 5. TAGA pairing based on the FHMQV protocol

In the worst case, the attacker could try to optimize the attack based on the sensor values sent by the aircraft: he could try to control the airflow in a way that maximizes the strain on the pipes without this being detected during service time but with a high risk that pipes burst during flight.

Our analysis of the prototype has shown that one either needs to refine TAGA by better protecting the TAGA channel, or by using an AKE protocol instead of the basic Diffie-Hellman exchange. In the following, we illustrate aspects of the latter refinement.

B. Refinement: Authenticated TAGA

The Authenticated Setting: In the setting of authenticated TAGA, every aircraft A has a long-term key pair (W_A, w_A), where W_A is the public key and w_A is the private key. Moreover, A holds a certificate for its public key W_A, which is issued by the airline $\mathcal{A}$ that owns A (or an entity commissioned by $\mathcal{A}$). We denote the certificate by $cert_{\mathcal{A}}(A, W_A, T_A, V_A)$, where T_A is the aircraft type of A, and V_A specifies the validity period of the certificate.

Analogously, every ground unit G has a long-term key pair (W_G, w_G), and a certificate for its public key W_G, which is issued by the airport $\mathcal{H}$ that harbours G (or an entity commissioned by $\mathcal{H}$). We denote the certificate by $cert_{\mathcal{H}}(G, W_G, S_G, V_G)$, where S_G is the service type of G and V_G is the validity period of the certificate.

We assume that every aircraft has installed the root certificates of those airports it intends to land at, and each ground unit has installed the root certificates of those airlines it is authorized to handle. For short notation, we often write a certificate $cert_{\mathcal{A}}(A, W_A, T_A, V_A)$ as $cert(A, W_A)$ when the issueing party, type of aircraft or service, and validity period are implicitly clear from the context.

Fig. 5 shows TAGA based on the *Fully Hashed Menezes-Qu-Vanstone protocol (FHMQV)* [7], [8]. For TAGA we include service and location into the key confirmation step. FHMQV is one of the strongest protocols regarding security, resilience and efficiency, and comes with a security proof. It satisfies all our secrecy and authentication requirements, i.e. Properties (1)–(4) of Table I, even when assuming that the attacker has full control of the TAGA channel. Our requirement 'Agreement with physical setup', i.e. Property (5), can also be guaranteed. Since we have included service and location into the key confirmation step the ground unit and aircraft will agree on service and location as part of the authentication guarantees. Then to obtain Property (5) the aircraft and ground unit only need to carry out a handshake of 'ready for service' messages once the secure channel is established.

The Threat of Long-term Key Compromise: While secure AKE protocols are designed to withstand an attacker who has full control of the network they are vulnerable to the threat of *long-term key compromises*. We say the attacker has obtained a *long-term key compromise (LTKC)* of the aircraft A if he has managed to get hold of credentials that authenticate A: a public/private key pair (W_A, w_A) and a valid certificate $cert(A, W_A)$, which asserts that W_A belongs to A. The definition for a ground unit G is analogous.

Given the LTKC of a party P, it is unavoidable that the attacker can impersonate P to other parties. In classical settings of AKE protocols this will typically impact on the resources of P, and only P, itself. However, in our setting a LTKC can have a wider impact. The following example shows how the attacker can use the LTKC of some aircraft A_I (possibly of an airline with key management of low security quality) to impersonate A_I to a ground unit that is physically connected to another aircraft A (possibly of an airline with key management of high security quality).

Example 4 (Impersonation to ground unit with LTKC of any aircraft). Let A_I be a real or non-existent aircraft of airline $\mathcal{A}_I$, and assume that the attacker has achieved a LTKC of A_I. Further, let A be an aircraft of airline $\mathcal{A}$, and G be a ground unit at airport $\mathcal{H}$ such that G provides service S to A during turnaround at parking slot L. In preparation, the attacker swaps his own counterfeit card C_I for the card of G's operator. Moreover, the attacker sets up NFC eavesdropping capability, and his own WLAN access point AP_I within range of L. Both AP_I and C_I are prepped with A_I's long-term credentials w_I and $cert(A_I, W_I)$, a fixed ephemeral key pair (r_I, R_I), and the SSID $ssid_I$ of the attacker's WLAN.

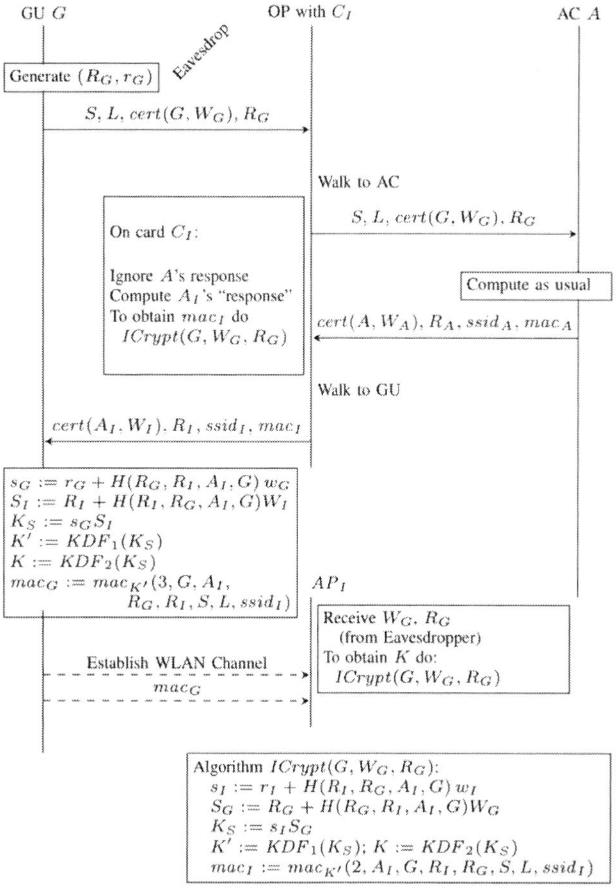

Fig. 6. Impersonation to ground unit with LTKC of any aircraft

Then the attacker can proceed as shown in Fig. 6: he simply establishes a key with G using A_I's credentials rather than those of A. Since A_I's ephemeral key pair can be fixed beforehand, the resulting session key can be computed independently on the card C_I, and the attacker's WLAN point AP_I respectively. The latter only needs to receive G's public keys by relay from the eavesdropping device.

Estimating the Safety Impact: The attacker has only obtained a Imp2SU connection compromise, and one may hope that this comes with less safety impact than MitM. However, Imp2SU still allows the attacker to feed any sensor values he likes to the ground unit while the ground unit thinks this information stems from the aircraft and adjusts the service correspondingly. The safety impact is potentially high for pre-conditioning.

Example 5 (Pre-Conditioning). The attacker feeds in airflow parameters and sensor values, and the ground unit will control the airflow based on this information. Since the air supply leads directly into the mixer unit of the aircraft this will take immediate effect without the aircraft itself having to open a valve or the like first. Crew or ground staff might notice that

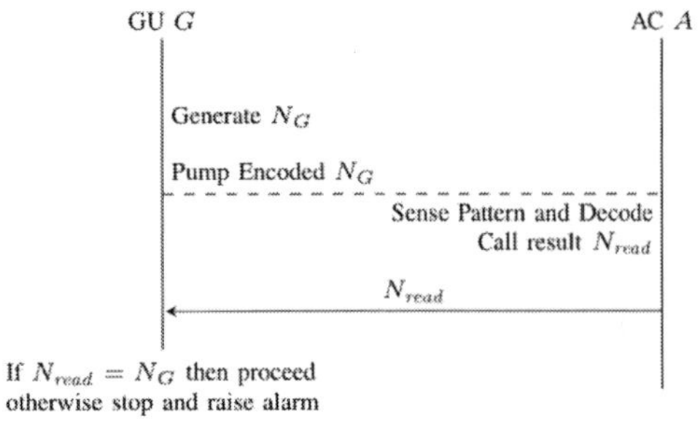

Fig. 7. Physical Challenge/Cyber Response

something is wrong and switch off the air supply manually. However, as explained in Example 3 damage can occur quickly and this might be too late. In contrast to the MitM attack, the attacker is not able to obtain sensor values sent by the aircraft, and, hence, he is not able to optimize the attack based on such information.

Given the potential safety impact and scale of the attack (given one LTKC) it is clear that a further refinement of the TAGA method is necessary. In particular, it is worth exploring measures that work on the ground service itself: one airline will not have much control over the security infrastructures managed by another. In addition, in our context of critical infrastructures one cannot write off that a state actor might take influence to obtain and abuse valid aircraft credentials of an airline in its realm.

C. Refinement: Including Mitigation Measures

We explore several ways of how to implement detection against Imp2SU (in the absence of MitM). The following measure translates the standard scheme of challenge/response authentication into the concept of *physical challenge/cyber response:* The ground unit sends a challenge via the physical connection, e.g. encoded in a pattern of pulsating flow, which the aircraft must answer via the cyber channel. Thereby the physical connection is directly bound into the key establishment method.

Example 6 (Physical Challenge/Cyber Response). Assume that the airpacks of the aircraft are equipped with mass airflow sensors that can detect a pattern of airflow changes and report it to its TAGA controller. Then a phase of physical challenge response can be included before the regular M2M communication starts as illustrated in Fig. 7. The ground unit G generates a random number of a fixed size, say N_G, and encodes this into a pattern of pulsating airflow. The aircraft A reads the physical signal by the airflow sensors and decodes it back into a number, say N_{read}. A then responds by sending N_{read} back to G via the cyber channel. G checks whether $N_{read} = N_G$. If this is true then G concludes that it speaks to the aircraft it is physically connected to: only this aircraft could have known N_G. If the numbers don't agree G stops and raises an alarm.

The space of nonces must be sufficiently large to reduce the risk of guessing attacks: even when the attacker cannot receive the physical signal he can always guess the nonce N_G and send it back via a cyber channel he has established with the ground unit by an impersonation attack. This brings about a trade-off between security and efficiency. For example: Say the physical channel allows a binary encoding of numbers in terms of high and low airflow (e.g. using stuffing to synchronize). Say an encoded bit requires 2 seconds to be transmitted, and a challenge shall maximally take 10 (or 20) seconds to be transmitted. Then one can use a space of 32 (or 1024) nonces, and the attacker has a 1/32 (or 1/1024) chance to guess correctly.

IV. Assessing and Mitigating the Safety Impact

We now describe a workflow of how the engineers of the maintenance procedure can iteratively assess the severity of impact, and explore and assess means to mitigate it. The workflow consists of the following activities. They can systematically be performed for each of the services, and for each of the relevant connection compromise states. In each of the steps simulation plays a crucial role.

1) Initial estimation and, if applicable, demonstration of the safety impact.
2) Refined analysis of the safety impact.
3) Exploration and assessment of mitigation measures.

Then iterate steps (2) and (3) until risk is mitigated to an acceptable level.

1) Initial Estimation of the Safety Impact: A first analysis of the safety impact is carried out. Usually, this can be done by hand by the engineers of the machines and maintenance process. This gives a first impression of whether a connection compromise state is critical or not. Our examples in Section III show that there can be differences across the services as well as across the connection compromise states.

It makes sense to carry out this initial step breadth-first for all services at hand. In this way one can learn early on if there are large differences between the risk levels across the services. Then one can e.g. partition them into several safety domains, or, mitigate the risk of individual services by additional measures.

Simulation can be an important tool at this stage to demonstrate the safety impact. This should not be underestimated: a demonstration is worth immensely more than a 1000 words when it comes to informing other team members or convincing management of the necessity of security measures (and their costs).

2) Refined Analysis of the Safety Impact: Many outcomes of the first phase will require a more refined analysis. In the positive case, when the initial estimation has delivered the result that the safety impact is controlled by existing safety mechanisms (c.f. Example 2) it might be important to submit this outcome to closer examination. This is so because safety measures such as backflow valves will not have been desigend to withstand malicicous intent, and the forces or patterns applied might be different when the system is under attack.

TABLE III
ATTACKER'S STRATEGIC GOALS

The attacker's strategic goal could be as follows: 1) create maximal damage while the maintenance process takes place, 2) create maximal damage during the operation of the vehicle after the maintenance process has taken place, 3) create maximal disruption, e.g. in terms of delays, equipment cost, locations affected, while a) the attack does not remain stealthy, b) the attack remains stealthy, c) the attack potential can be demonstrated without being carried out (in view of ransomware attacks).

In the negative case, when the initial estimation has delivered the result that safety impact is to be expected it might be important to explore the attack capabilites in more detail, e.g. to determine whether the attack will only lead to disruption or put passengers at risk (c.f. Example 3).

For this phase we assume that the service under investigation is already modelled in a tool such as Stateflow/Simulink. The model then only needs to be extended to integrate the respective connection compromise state. We suggest to provide one channel component for each of the connection compromise states in addition to the original uncrompromised channel component. Then during evaluation one can switch between the different channel models as required.

The question remains of how to choose the input values for the attack simulations. E.g. to assess the Imp2SU state, which sensor inputs shall the attacker model communicate to the model of the service unit? At first sight, it might seem plausible to use the fault models typically used in safety analysis such as 'stuck at' or 'random'. However, this will not sufficiently reflect that during an attack the values are chosen by a purposeful attacker. We propose instead to identify the strategic goals an attacker might have, and to choose the system inputs accordingly. In Table III we show a first draft of such goals. We have separated out two dimensions: the type of damage an attacker intends to cause, and the attack mode, e.g. whether the attack shall remain stealthy or not. Note that, in particular for stealthy attacks, the input patterns might not be obvious. Then simulation also has an important role to play to find and optimize the system parameters accordingly.

It is a joint task for safety engineers and security engineers in cooperation with members of agencies such as the BSI (Bundesamt für Sicherheit in der Informationstechnik), the relevant authority in Germany, to assess the likelihood of such attacks: the first group can assess the necessary resources (e.g. knowledge, access to equipment) for an attack category, while the latter can assess whether corresponding groups with the respective strategic goals are able to obtain these resources.

3) Exploration and Assessment of Mitigation Measures: In Section III-C we have seen by example that measures that act on the physical part of the service can play an important role to mitigate the impact when key establishment fails. The following measures might be options to protect against Imp2SU or even MitM:

- *Physical Challenge/Cyber Response (only against Imp2SU):* as described in Example 6.
- *Time-based Detection (only against Imp2SU):* Due to the interweaving with the physical setup an attacker who carries out an Imp2SU attack will typically need to initiate a fake key establishment session with the vehicle (c.f. Example 4) as part of the attack. This session will never be completed, and hence, the vehicle could raise an alarm when a session is still pending after an unusally long time. Operators could then check what is going on, and, e.g. deactivate the service unit before damage occurs.
- *Safety Check and Safety Alert:* The vehicle or service unit could integrate sensors to check whether system variables such as temperature or pressure are about to cross safety limits. Then an alarm could be raised, and operators could deactivate the machine from which the danger emanates. Note that it is not possible to deactivate the machine automatically: it is the machine opposite to the one that raises the alarm that will need to be switched off. Moreover, since the communication channel is thought to be under attack it is not possible to reliably send a deactivation request message to the peer machine either.
- *Physics-based Attack Detection:* Physics-based attack detection employs a physical model of the normal behaviour of the system to monitor whether real-time measurements of system variables are consistent with the expected behaviour of the system [9], [10]. This concept could be applied in our context as follows. As with the previous measure the vehicle is equipped with sensors that take real-time measurements of system variables. A digital twin of the control of the service unit models the expected behaviour under the assumption that the service unit indeed receives the sensor values the vehicle communicates. If there is a deviation to the actual behaviour then an alarm will be raised. As with the safety check method, it is the opposite machine, here the service unit, that needs to be deactivated, and hence, this has to be carried out by operators.

Simulation can either be part of the measure itself as with cyber-physical attack detection in form of a digital twin or it can play a crucial role to validate the measure. There are several facets here: first, to validate whether the physics behind the method will indeed work. Second, to simulate and validate the actions of ground personnel in case of an alarm, e.g. to estimate the time it takes for them to deactive the respective machine. And third, to validate whether the time between the alarm and the deactivation is sufficiently short to reduce risk before damage is caused. Finally, co-simulation can be used for an overall validation. Again, simulation can also be used for parameter optimization. For any attack detection system it will be important to consider the evaluation criteria considered in [10]: the trade-off between the maximum deviation of critical system variables per time unit imposed by undetected attacks, and the expected time between false alarms.

V. Conclusions and Future Work

We hope this paper has demonstrated that a key establishment method can be systematically developed and validated for security and safety, and that simulation plays an important role in this process. Of course, the activities described here can be followed by bench/live tests, and formal verification where necessary. In particular, we will investigate whether and how statistical model-checking [11] can be made use of in the tool-chain: to be able to verify integrated safetey and security properties such as: "Safety mitigation kicks in before attack causes harm with probability $> P$".

References

[1] C. Boyd, A. Mathuria, and D. Stebila, *Protocols for Authentication and Key Establishment*, 2nd ed. Springer Publishing Company, Incorporated, 2020.

[2] M. Li, W. Lou, and K. Ren, "Secure device pairing," in *Encyclopedia of Cryptography and Security*. Springer US, 2011, pp. 1111–1115.

[3] S. Mirzadeh, H. Cruickshank, and R. Tafazolli, "Secure device pairing: A survey," *IEEE Communications Surveys & Tutorials*, vol. 16, no. 1, pp. 17–40, 2014.

[4] M. Fomichev, F. Álvarez, D. Steinmetzer, P. Gardner-Stephen, and M. Hollick, "Survey and systematization of secure device pairing," *IEEE Communications Surveys & Tutorials*, vol. 20, no. 1, pp. 517–550, 2018.

[5] G. Lowe, "A hierarchy of authentication specification," in *10th Computer Security Foundations Workshop (CSFW '97), June 10-12, 1997*. IEEE Computer Society, 1997, pp. 31–44.

[6] B. Schmidt, S. Meier, C. Cremers, and D. Basin, "Automated analysis of Diffie-Hellman protocols and advanced security properties," in *25th IEEE Computer Security Foundations Symposium, CSF 2012*. IEEE, 2012, pp. 78–94.

[7] A. P. Sarr, P. Elbaz-Vincent, and J.-C. Bajard, "A secure and efficient authenticated Diffie–Hellman protocol," in *Public Key Infrastructures, Services and Applications*. Springer, 2010, pp. 83–98.

[8] A. P. Sarr and P. Elbaz-Vincent, "On the security of the (F)HMQV protocol," in *Progress in Cryptology – AFRICACRYPT 2016*. Springer International Publishing, 2016, pp. 207–224.

[9] J. Giraldo, D. Urbina, A. Cardenas, J. Valente, M. Faisal, J. Ruths, N. O. Tippenhauer, H. Sandberg, and R. Candell, "A survey of physics-based attack detection in cyber-physical systems," *ACM Comput. Surv.*, vol. 51, no. 4, jul 2018. [Online]. Available: https://doi.org/10.1145/3203245

[10] D. I. Urbina, J. A. Giraldo, A. A. Cardenas, N. O. Tippenhauer, J. Valente, M. Faisal, J. Ruths, R. Candell, and H. Sandberg, "Limiting the impact of stealthy attacks on industrial control systems," in *Proceedings of the 2016 ACM SIGSAC Conference on Computer and Communications Security*, ser. CCS '16. New York, NY, USA: Association for Computing Machinery, 2016, p. 1092–1105. [Online]. Available: https://doi.org/10.1145/2976749.2978388

[11] E. M. Clarke and P. Zuliani, "Statistical model checking for cyber-physical systems," in *Automated Technology for Verification and Analysis*, T. Bultan and P.-A. Hsiung, Eds. Berlin, Heidelberg: Springer Berlin Heidelberg, 2011, pp. 1–12.